THE
HONEST
TODDLER

A Child's Guide to Parenting

Written under the supervision of

Bunmi Laditan

SCRIBNER

New York   London   Toronto   Sydney   New Delhi

SCRIBNER
A Division of Simon & Schuster, Inc.
1230 Avenue of the Americas
New York, NY 10020

Copyright © 2013 by Olubunmi Laditan

First Scribner hardcover edition May 2013

SCRIBNER and design are registered trademarks of The Gale Group, Inc.,
used under license by Simon & Schuster, Inc., the publisher of this work.

For information about special discounts for bulk purchases,
please contact Simon & Schuster Special Sales at 1-866-506-1949
or business@simonandschuster.com.

The Simon & Schuster Speakers Bureau can bring authors to your live event.
For more information or to book an event contact the Simon & Schuster Speakers Bureau
at 1-866-248-3049 or visit our website at www.simonspeakers.com.

DESIGNED BY ERICH HOBBING

Manufactured in the United States of America

1   3   5   7   9   10   8   6   4   2

ISBN 978-1-4767-3371-5
ISBN 978-1-4767-3372-2 (ebook)

To Etienne: *Je t'aime.*
Merci d'être mon rocher
et parfois, mon oreiller.

To my children,
you're my finest work, and I love you
way past the moon and back.
Now please calm down.

Contents

CONTENTS

The
Honest
Toddler

Introduction

Name: Honest Toddler.
Status: Not potty trained, not trying.
Age: This many.
Likes: Cake, running, shows, games, and red drink.
Dislikes: Naps, bedtime, unsolicited eye contact, quinoa, pants,
   and all forms of discipline.

If you are holding this book in your hand, whether you bought it with money or just picked it up and ran to the car, you've made a good choice. Toddlers are misunderstood and the one in your life is probably disappointed in you. Read this book if you want to get better at what should be your number one priority: making your small child happy.

Don't skip pages, this isn't a bedtime story (yeah, we know) but a manual that will revolutionize your life. You're welcome in advance.

P.S. Grandmas: You're doing great. Keep it up. (Love you.)

Dear Honest Toddler,

My two-year-old is terrified of the vacuum cleaner, but I need to clean. What can I do!?

—Messy in Bakersfield, California

Dear Messy,

Kill the vacuum cleaner with a knife. You can always wipe down the house with damp newspaper.

Lots of love, HT

♦ ♦ ♦

Dear HT,

My toddler has been acting like a bit of an animal lately. Ripping paper money, peeing on the outside plants . . . we're at our wits' end. Any advice?

—Losing Steam in Atlanta

Hi Losing Steam,

When toddlers act out, it means they aren't getting enough love or red drink. Try increasing both, and while you are losing things, you could start with the judgy tone.

Sincerely, HT

1

"Why Did You Do That?":
The Ins and Outs of Toddler Behavior
and How to Leave It Alone

Listening ears, gentle hands, inside voices. If you're an adult, you've probably used these terms three to four hundred times in the last ten minutes. Question: Do you know what "minding your business" means? It means letting your child's spirit remain free. Your number one responsibility as a volunteer caregiver is to keep the unbroken crackers and full-strength juice coming. Rather than trying to fix your blessing, you should try to understand your sweet baby's behavior so that you can provide more attentive customer service. This chapter is dedicated to helping you become a better unpaid intern to your toddler.

Tantrums

There's a very dirty word that is commonly used to describe the mild outbursts of emotion that toddlers display from time to time. That word is TANTRUM. Not only is this descriptor condescending, it releases the party responsible (you) for said "tantrum."

Wrong: Oh, Maya's just throwing a tantrum. Let's stand here with arms folded like despots and wait for it to pass.

Right: Maya is lying on her back in this crowded restaurant, screaming and trying to kick everyone within roundhouse distance. I wonder how I failed her?

Do you see how language creates toddler bias? From now on, we'll be throwing the word "tantrum" in the metaphorical outside trash and replacing it with "loud response."

Last week I shared a loud response in our local Linens 'n Things. Don't be confused by the name of this retail outlet. There are no Things. Just Linens. After forty-six hours of wandering this textile purgatory, I felt a volcano erupt in my middle back. The last thing I remember is trying to rip an Egyptian-cotton duvet with my teeth and releasing my bowels on a couple of crushed-velvet throw pillows before running for my life. My behavior was a response, not a random occurrence.

Parents, if you wish to gain the respect of your toddler, the first thing you need to do is own your mistakes. For instance, if my parents and I had been at the toy store eating delicious and nutritious ice-cream sundaes, like I'd asked, we could have spent the money that went toward those pee-pee pillows on the new toys I desperately need. Do you see?

Research: Go out into the field and observe loud responses firsthand in order to get a sense of why and how they occur. A popular place for scouting is the grocery store between four and five thirty P.M. While you're most likely to find an outburst occurring in nearly every aisle, for the best lessons, visit the cereal/snack/chip lane. The market is a land mine for parent/toddler conflict due to overuse of the dirty word "NO." Also, most people don't realize this, but green vegetables emit a field of negative energy that contributes to the sadness and rage children feel while food shopping.

Combine these factors with post-nap confusion, coupled with a literal wall of delicious but unavailable refined carbohydrates, and yes, you guessed it: loud response.

Right now you're asking yourself, "Wait a minute, why don't these parents just open a box of Ritz crackers right in the grocery store so their child will be happy? What's wrong with that?"

Nothing. There's nothing wrong with that. It is only the stubbornness of adults that prevents them from tearing apart a box of cereal at both ends so their child might have the strength to make it through the late afternoon.

They say pride comes before a fall. In this case, it comes before loud and, honestly, quite impressive responses on behalf of toddlers around the world. Parents, don't fool yourselves. Loud responses cannot be prevented by inCARTceration. It's fairly easy for an experienced toddler to erupt in emotional pain and low blood sugar–fueled angst while secured in the front half of a shopping cart. Our arms are free to slap. Our feet can still connect with your kneecaps. Our heads can roll around in figure-eight formation while we release screams so gut-wrenching that strangers correctly assume you're doing it all wrong.

The only solution is to open the Goldfish, yogurt (eating yogurt with hands is okay), or family-sized package of licorice right then and there. The evil voices in your head might be whispering things like "Don't give in, don't cave." Silence the chatter and bring your awareness to the present. And *buy* presents. Buy them for your toddler. Shower him with food gifts.

One of my favorite loud responses to watch is the one that takes place when a parent tries to prematurely remove a child from the park. Everyone knows that we have an obesity epidemic on our hands, so why not let your budding athlete exercise until after the sun has gone down and the prime-time television lineup has begun (that's the real reason you're going home, isn't it?). I admire children who literally go the extra mile by engaging their parents in a mad chase around the play structure to prevent the scoop 'n' go. In my mind, I scream "Run, Forrest, run!" as Mom or Dad tries desperately to catch their sprinting young gazelle. It's a beautiful thing.

Outbursts are not to be feared. They're to be prevented, and only you have the power to do that. The next time you think about walking out of Starbucks with a grande nonfat extra-hot hazelnut mocha for yourself and no giant chocolate-chip cookie for your patient cherubesque darling, consider the consequences. Are you ready for a throwdown? Because we are.

Note: Loud responses are between you and your child. Taking photos for Facebook or discussing them with other parents is unnecessary and a violation of privacy laws. Bringing up a loud response long after it has occurred is emotional abuse. Once the squall has passed, wipe the sweat off your face and move on.

- -

Homework: Go to the grocery store with your child at five thirty P.M. When the loud response starts, scream, "EVERYONE SHUT UP, I NEED TO HELP MY CHILD." Then open four large bags of chips and a juice box. Let your child feast.

- -

Deadweight/Going Boneless

Adults, do you enjoy running errands? That's fantastic. Go on your own time. There isn't a toddler in the world who wants to accompany you on a thirty-six-store whirlwind of boring. The worst part about running errands is that actual running is discouraged. And we're never rushing out to pick up Popsicles or glow sticks; it's mostly dry cleaning and cupboard liners.

You already know that loud responses are your fault. There is another toddler phenomenon that you bring upon yourself. Deadweight, otherwise known as Going Boneless, is when your toddler opens a valve within his or her brain that converts hard bone minerals into bubble gum and increases body weight by 70 to 80 percent.

Activating deadweight is very simple. Every toddler has his unique style, but I prefer a straightforward approach.

How It Starts

1. **Slow motion:** Your toddler will begin walking as if each step is physically painful. I like to thrust my shoulders forward, causing my knuckles to graze the ground.
2. **Verbal indicators:** "I'm tired. I can't walk." Did you hear that? You are now at a crossroads. Smart parents will immediately pick up their toddler and find the nearest Cinnabon. Stubborn parents will soon be humiliated in public. Saying things like "C'mon, let's go, we're almost there" feels like a slap in the face to the child, who you say means something to you.

BAM! It'll be sudden. You'll look back and spot your child on the ground. First, you'll be shocked; your eyes will dart around to see if anyone is watching. Oh, trust me, they are.

I love the way parents always try to act like they can't believe what they're seeing. "What? My otherwise obedient child is lying on the sidewalk like a discarded flyer? Heavens, no!" LOL, you're not fooling anybody.

Time to make it right.

Here's What **NOT** to Do:

DO NOT try to pull your innocent child up by one arm unless you've been dying to visit your local emergency room and explain to the nurses why baby's arm is dislocated. You like jail?

DO NOT contort your face like a Disney witch and angry-whisper in your child's ear. You look funnier than you could ever imagine. But nobody's laughing.

DO NOT make wild threats, because you sound crazy.

When toddlers Go Boneless, they can't hear the world around them. Only harps and angels. And the angels are saying, "Stay down, baby, stay down." Don't bother making ice-cream promises. It's too late for that. The only solution is to airlift your toddler out. Your child is no longer capable of using her muscles. You broke them when you broke her trust. Be sure to support your toddler's flopping head.

Remember: This is your doing.

- -

Homework: (1) Practice running errands online. **(2)** Next time you're out of the house and your child's legs stop working, immediately rush to his side and pick him up. If you have too many bags to hold or a stroller, leave everything in the street.

- -

Listening Ears

If you've ever asked a child in your care to put on his or her listening ears, this section is for you. Even if your intentions are pure and you need your toddler's attention for the purpose of asking what type of cake to prepare for lunch, it's time to throw this insipid term out the car window.

Before writing this chapter, I interviewed a prominent pediatrician. After she was done poking at my bare stomach (lawsuit pending), she revealed to me that listening ears do not exist. You might feel like a fool. This is normal. Forgive yourself and keep reading.

Let's get to the heart of the matter. When you ask your toddler to put on fake ears, what you're really trying to say is "LISTEN TO ME RIGHT NOW." Surprise! Your toddler hears you. He or she is just practicing what we in the toddler world call "selective acknowledgment."

Your child probably does not have a hearing problem. There's no need to snap your fingers close to your kid's ears and watch for corresponding blinks. We can hear you; we are just not interested.

Allow me to set the scene: You're in the kitchen sweeping up nothing and decide your child is having too much fun in another room without you. Loneliness hits you in the face, and you begin to yell your toddler's name over and over like some kind of entitled foghorn. Nothing happens, so you morph into Quasimodo from *The Hunchback of Notre-Dame* and storm into the family room, where your child is building the most beautiful block cityscape the world has ever seen. Standing five feet away from your future award-winning architect, you loudly say his name over and over. Anger rises in your frail body when your toddler doesn't even flinch. You suddenly realize how annoying you sound and walk away.*

> **Wrong Question:** *Why is it that my child seems to block out my voice?*

> **Right Question:** *What am I saying that is so offensive/irrelevant that my child has no choice but to ignore me?*

There are four conversation topics that will always cause you to be on the receiving end of selective acknowledgment. If being heard is important to you, avoid these topics. Life is so easy.

Four No-No Convos

1. Meal Calls

"Noah, it's time to eat more quinoa or fish larvae—who knows, because they look exactly the same." "Tali, wash your hands for lunch, even though these shrimp tacos will probably cause you more physical harm than germs will."

If the breakfast, lunch, or dinner you've prepared smells good enough, you won't need to bark an announcement. Selective acknowledgment is a cue that you need to throw away the stuffed

---

*Toddler-approved ending.

cabbage (why?) and dial 1–800 Plain Cheese Pizza. Do not expect your toddler to come running for a casserole that looks like a waste of cheese and smells like a bouquet of resentment. Say it with me: "toast."

2. General Check-ins

"Felix, what are you doing in there? Felix? Felix!?" "Stephen, your silence indicates that you've found something interesting to do. Please confirm or deny, because I say so."

You sound so needy, you have no idea. If you, the adult, find yourself in a room different from your child, it is your responsibility to check to make sure all is well. During their rounds, prison guards go from cell to cell. The inmates aren't required to scream verbal assurances all day while their captors browse Pinterest for wine-cork crafts. Take the .01-mile stroll. Bring a water bottle if the distance proves too taxing.*

3. Formalities and Greetings

"Robert, come say hi to Aunt Betty on the phone." "Your friends are leaving your birthday party, Rebecca, come say goodbye!"

What? No. Just no. These people will survive without a forced smile, wave, or salutation. Toddlers know that adults spend 80 percent of their lives pretending to care about people who matter very little to them (Facebook), and we're committed to avoiding a similar fate. If you wish to extend words of fake kindness to a person, do so, but don't expect your toddler to look up.

4. Transitions

"Hey, Isabella, drop everything and break the concentration you've built up since forever. Time to try something new and probably undesirable." There's nothing a toddler hates more than the next

---

*So lazy.

thing. If your end goal is to change tasks, even if it's from gluing beans on a piece of paper to gluing pinwheel pasta on a piece of paper, please prepare yourself for, at best, selective acknowledgment or, at worst, a loud response.

When you notice your special toddler engaging in selective acknowledgment, get excited, because it means she is most likely very gifted. You may be tempted to put a hand on your child's shoulder or do an upper-arm grab to get her attention, but really, that's bordering on assault. If assault is part of who you want to be, by all means.

There's even more good news. Selective acknowledgment has a partner skill known as hyperawareness. I can hear someone open a bag of chips through seven solid brick walls in the middle of a thunderstorm *while sleeping*. Please hold your applause.

Important note: You may have noticed an extension of selective acknowledgment called the "blank stare." Savvy toddlers use the blank stare as a way of letting you know that they are not connecting with your information or that they have temporarily abandoned present reality for a more entertaining dimension within their psyches. I blank-stare at least three to five times a day. It DOES NOT help to crouch three inches from your child's face and repeat your query ad nauseam. If your child's eyes are glassy and her mouth is slightly agape, know that you are very important and your message will be answered in the order it was received.

Inside Voices vs. Outside Voices

Outside voices win. The end.

- -

Homework: Stop acting like you know everything.

- -

"Whining"

When adults talk about being tired or the price of onions (nobody asked you to buy them), it's called complaining. When Adele does it, it's Grammys. But when your toddler musically communicates dissatisfaction, you label it "whining." It's time for adults to acknowledge whining as a legitimate form of speech.

Wrong:
Amazing Child: Moooomyyyyy, I neeed heeeelp.

Cold-as-Ice Lady: I can't hear you when you talk like that. Just kidding, I can, but self-righteousness is in style, and I want to be impressive.

Right:
Amazing Child: Mooomyyyy, I neeed heeeelp.

Beautiful Lady: Oh my goodness, how did I let this situation get to the point where you feel so frustrated? At least I'm here now. How can I serve you my angel/master?

When your toddler is forced to extend vowels, that means she is upset, and unless it's illegal to be sad, you have no ground to stand on. In some cultures, whining is considered a signal that a child is dangerously low on M&M's. Let that idea sink in.

Whining is actually an instrument, much like a violin or a drum. When you stop thinking about whining as a problem and start dancing to the melody of your child's needs, life will reward you with tasks. If, after all of this knowledge, you still don't enjoy whining, try harder to anticipate your toddler's wants.

Toddlers often whine when they are bored, because their toys are no longer entertaining. You can remedy this by replenishing the toy supply every week. Do not throw out the old ones; just let the pile grow. Always have something fun—like a PEZ dispenser or Silly Putty—in your pocket to prevent sadness in your child's heart. Keep some Skittles in a small box around your neck to treat emergency hunger. Being prepared can go a long way toward preventing whining.

Homework: Wait for your child to start whining. It won't take long. When it begins, crouch down to your toddler's height (with a smile on your face) and say, "I'm bad. How can I help you?" while tucking a stick of gum into her hand. Watch your child's face relax. This is called "family."

Gentle Hands

I'm going to be honest and say that I'm not 100 percent sure what gentle hands are. I know they have to do with not making animals cry. My friend's goldfish was the victim of a gentle-hands accident after it failed a hug test. This is in no way anyone's fault.

Sometimes toddlers love hard. You should praise your child for having a heart of gold and a fist of steel.

Most adults push the idea of gentle hands on their toddlers for the sake of preserving the precious IKEA items in their home. Herein lies the dilemma. What's more important to you as a parent: owning intact compressed-wood furniture or developing the strength and self-esteem of a child? I hope the answer was simple. If it wasn't, you have a lot to think about and should probably go sit in the dark until you get your priorities straight.

There's one more false application of gentle hands that I want to touch on. (Did you see what I did there? With the "touch." Did you see that? It's a pun. Start the sentence again.)

Other children, from time to time, may earn themselves a slight tap in the face, head, or middle-back area for grabbing a toy that does not belong to them or wearing a shirt that your child feels should be hers. *There's nothing wrong with this.* You'll be tempted to step in loudly and make a scene, but you're embarrassing yourself. We call this Tot Justice. Let the children slap it out. If your child loses, that just means you need to practice the ancient art of ka-ra-tay at home.

Gentle hands violate the number one rule of being a toddler, which is "breaking." Why did you take all of those prenatal vitamins if raising a weakling was your end goal?

Sharing

Sharing is stupid. I'm sorry, I got ahead of myself. Sharing is a hot-button issue in many parenting books. You'll be happy to know that they've got it all wrong. It's time for you to put on your thinking cap and use common sense. Everything in the world is divided up based on who owns it. We use the words "yours" and, more important, "mine" to label these items. There is a word called "ours," but it's only used to refer to things that are difficult to put in a bag, like sunlight, air, or the wetlands.

Sand toys, trucks, dolls, and food can all be owned.

Even though it sounds ridiculous, many adults believe that because children don't have formal employment, all of their possessions must be nonproprietary. This form of communism is not only dangerous but 100 percent no.

> **Wrong:** *Sadie, it looks like Henry wants to play with your LEGOs. Why don't you give up your dreams and let him destroy everything?*

> **Right:** *Sadie, it looks like Henry wants to play with your LEGOs. Move aside while I throw him out of this house.*

"Why Did You Do That?"

Seventy percent of all toddler-on-toddler violence comes from sharing. Eighty-six percent of toddler illness is a direct result of sharing. Behind errands, sharing is the number one cause of loud responses. Do you still think it's a good idea?

Sharing is a socially accepted form of theft and needs to be abolished. A sense of philanthropy will develop naturally in your child once he has a clear sense of what is his. The belief that all things belong to everyone make growing a charitable heart impossible, because why does one need to give if everyone already has potential access to everything? I believe the word I'm looking for is BOOM.

The park is not the former Soviet Union. Before you show up, make sure your toddler has a basket full of sand toys in working condition so that he isn't tempted. A playdate is not an opportunity for your child to put her hands or eyes on someone else's treasures.* You have been invited to share in the general atmosphere. Do not, I repeat, do not make yourself at home. Mi casa es mi casa.

Even in sticky situations, adults have the responsibility to help toddlers determine ownership rights. Consider this scenario: Two toddlers are sitting at a small round table, drawing. There is only one blue crayon. Both toddlers need the blue crayon. What do you do? Nothing. Both toddlers' lives are over. Why do you have only one blue crayon? Do you enjoy seeing children in pain? Just put on a movie. It's too late.

Parents, please be honest with yourselves. Do you like sharing? If a strange woman or man knocked on your door and asked to borrow your vehicle, how would you feel? Mothers, everyone sees how you guard your purse, as if it's full of gold coins and chardonnay rather than toddler socks and receipts. Daddies, you clench that remote control as if it's the only thing keeping your heart beating. It's time to admit that sharing hurts everybody.

Exemption: Give me all the things.

Homework: Slow down on the bad ideas.

Lying

Everybody lies. Toddlers just don't apologize for it. When you think about it, a lie is the truth with a funny hat on. The next time your toddler lies to your face, giggle and smile. Share a few hugs and know that you probably just asked the wrong question. The number one reason toddlers spin reality is to avoid trouble. When you ask questions like "Laura, did you poo in the fireplace?" what do you expect to happen? We both know Laura did and that you've already judged her for it. What does she have to lose by fabricating a tall tale?

You may be interested to learn that questioning a toddler without a lawyer present is a violation of human rights.

Parents all over the world try convincing their children that the truth is king when truth is nothing but a common jester. At any given time, there are infinite realities floating around. If your toddler plucks one from the air and it doesn't happen to match yours, is that anyone's fault? The right answer is "no."

Did you hit your sister with a foam bat?

Did you pee-pee on the couch?

Did you eat my flowers?

So many questions! It's no wonder your sweet toddler is confused. It seems as if most of these queries are leading up to a time-out, so don't be surprised if your toddler isn't even around to answer them. Don't check behind the drapes, because he's not there.

Since practicing what you preach is important, before you ask your toddler to commit to the truth, you may want to walk a mile in those soft-soled shoes. Daddies, perhaps you'd like to share how you really feel about Mama's five-bean casserole? Or admit that you actually do know how to operate the dishwasher? Mommy, maybe it's time to stop buying precooked rotisserie chicken, throwing the container in the outside garbage, and passing it off as some kind of family recipe? Just sayin'.

Testing Limits

You've just broken your toddler's heart and told her NO in a voice that sounds like a cross between *Aladdin*'s Jafar and the witch from *Tangled*. Before you start wagging your finger, your toddler stands up to evil and defies you.

Typical Adult: *I asked my toddler not to touch the remote control, but she did, and it exploded in her hand.*

First, lower your voice. Second, relax your expectations. And by "relax," I mean eliminate. When your child openly disobeys you, it is called courage. Measure your body with a ruler. Now measure your toddler's. Who is bigger? The fact that David stood up to Goliath indicates that your toddler is a person of character. I'm sure you are familiar with the term "bully."

The scariest thing you can do when your toddler bends the law is whisper like a serpent between unmoving teeth. There's no reason for that. One hundred percent uncalled for, in fact. If you're also two inches from your child's face, consider yourself a failure, hang up your coat, and please notify Grandma that you retire, effective immediately.

It may not be easy to watch your child jump on the couch or put his hand in a bowl of gravy after you explicitly told him not to, but the great news is that nobody is requiring you to watch. Open some of that wine you enjoy so much and have a seat. Avert your gaze. Think of the last few items you've pinned on Pinterest. Fantasize about Etsy. Plan your next public Facebook argument. You can go anywhere in your imagination. Just don't go physically, because that would be upsetting.

Below are some positive affirmations for you to practice daily. Say them aloud in the shower, but not too loud, because your toddler is probably standing right there, supervising your body washing.

Positive Affirmations:
- "Yes" means "love." I say yes. I am love.
- DEFiance is DEFinitely not a problem.
- Today I am planting a garden of happiness. The seeds are my closed mouth.

It has taken me months but I am finally on my way to opening up the lines of communication in my home through yelling. Let the dictator inside you melt into a puddle of dirty water around your feet. Then lay down a towel and clean up the mess. After that, take your child to an indoor play center. Not the free kind; one that costs money. Come home and serve hot dogs with no bun and pretzels as a side dish. Then play until you both fall asleep in the family room. What a beautiful day that was.

- -

Homework: Write down all of your household rules on a piece of paper. Eat it. I'm serious. It's not as bad as you think. Rip it into strips if you need to, but get it done.

- -

Note: Your personal frustrations with your toddler's lifestyle are no reason to ruin her relationship with Santa. That's called snitchery and is frowned upon in most social circles. Grandma is also uninterested in your wild tales, so please keep them to yourself. Spreading news about others is gossip and a sign of a weak moral compass.

Risk Taking

Have you heard of cliff jumping? No? It's a sport invented by toddlers wherein you find the highest place you can reach and believe deeply that gravity doesn't apply to you. If you've ever seen your child climb on the kitchen table and throw himself off or roll head-first down a flight of stairs, then you know that self-preservation means little to us. We're "act first, think never" adventurers.

You can help enhance the experience by making it more interesting. Invest in a smoke machine. When your toddler is in Destruction Mode, atmosphere is everything. Mood music can take an experience to cinematic heights. Commission a costume designer to create a superhero bodysuit and matching cape. A mask would be a wonderful gift and sign of support.

It's impossible to know how many toddlers have jumped from the top of the playground jungle gym while their parents stood out of reach, mouths agape in silent screams. Unless you plan to hold your child's hand while she explores the entire world, you have to accept that she hails from a long line of superheroes and needs to spend her formative years training for an inevitable battle to save Planet Earth. Do you think Superman's parents ever had him on one of those backpack leashes? Absolutely not.

You may not know this, but toddlers are invincible. If your child is wearing enough Band-Aids (mini-shields), nothing can touch him.

Note: The only time a toddler can be injured is when a parent views the accident. The gaze of a parent is like kryptonite and immediately weakens the child. I myself have rebounded from countless spills. I've BOUNCED off hardwood floors and walked away from incidents involving walls that came out of nowhere. If trees could talk, they would tell you how I run into them on a regular basis. But the one time I knew I was being watched falling off a two-foot-tall slide, I was unable to walk without assistance for days, despite no physical signs of damage.

Mood Swings

Please take the short survey below.

1. My toddler can go from uncontrollable sobbing to slightly frightening hyena laughter in a matter of milliseconds:
   a. Never
   b. Rarely
   c. Sometimes
   d. Often
   e. It's happening right now
2. My sweet baby is prone to bouts of rage that seem unprovoked:
   a. Never
   b. Rarely
   c. Sometimes
   d. Often
   e. It's happening right now
3. My angel has kissed me gently and slapped me across the face within the same five-minute period:
   a. Yes
   b. No

Use the answers above to determine if your child may suffer from mood swings. Don't worry, he is not alone, and the treatment is noninvasive. You wouldn't blame someone with a cold for sneezing, so when your toddler giggles one second and uses urine as a weapon the next, it's not a big deal.

Most toddler mood swings can be cured with simple board-certified* medicinal formulas. The good news is that it's easy to make these cures at home.

*Not board-certified.

Anger Solvent

Mix together 3 tablespoons of coconut oil, 1 teaspoon of dried bay leaves, and 1/3 cup mineral water. Rub it on your own head until you feel humble. Gently place a gummy bear in your toddler's mouth. Watch your child for signs of dissipating anger. Repeat with a new gummy bear every two minutes, no matter what.

Homeopathic Stability Pills

Dehydrate an entire bottle of liquid Tylenol until it resembles fruit leather. Put it on a high shelf. Acquire a family-sized tub of Rolos or any other chocolate-covered caramels. Walk slowly toward your toddler without looking her directly in the eye. With your head lowered, drop the candy offering at your toddler's feet. Whisper "I'm so sorry" as you back away.

Child-Calming Dust

Spend two hundred dollars on essential oils. Cry over your poor choices. Empty a bag of mini-marshmallows into a large pot. Stir until it becomes powder. Sprinkle the dust liberally into your child's mouth when she shows signs of distress. Keep a large Ziploc bag of dust on your person at all times. This is organic.

Cry-Be-Gone Spray

Make a simple syrup of brown sugar, maple syrup, candy canes, and water. Add sprinkles. Allow to cool, and pour into a spray bottle. When your toddler seems out of sorts, spray all around her, focusing on the mouth area.

You may not see any immediate changes in your toddler, but you're not the boss of the world or a scientist, so just keep at it. Hugs can go only so far. These time-honored recipes are full of wisdom and healing power. Most biologists agree that sugar helps stabilize minds. If someone told you different, check his pockets for a card that says "certified liar," because he most certainly is one.

Regressing

Have you experienced this phenomenon? One day your toddler is walking around like the king of the jungle, ripping up mail and pushing friends, but the next day she has forgotten how to use a spoon, no longer has words, and needs to be held round the clock. What happened? Why is your big kid acting like a big baby?

Most doctors agree that regression occurs when a child has been infected with Infant Disease. Infant Disease is when a baby who can't walk steals the life force from a powerful older child through required sharing or attention theft. Parents, ask yourself: Have you had any newborns in your home lately? Last week my mother hosted a baby shower, which, if you don't already know, is a celebration for a child who hasn't even been born. There were three babies in attendance who skillfully used their knowledge of the dark arts to capture everyone's attention. My mother was not immune to their witchcraft and held them for at least fifteen minutes each, despite my loud response. I suffered from Infant Disease for the next two and a half days and am just beginning to feel like myself.

There is a very simple precaution that you can take to keep your toddler safe from crook babies.

Avoid Infants

Don't be tempted to look at these living bags of oatmeal when you pass them in the grocery store. Do not "ooh" and definitely do not "ahh" when you see them lying on tarps, staring up at the sky at the park. There's nothing special about a child who can't go anywhere without a blanket over her legs. Everyone knows that most children under one are liars, so there is no reason to admire them.

Homework: The next time a friend asks you to hold her baby, pretend like you don't mind, then at the last minute, scream loudly. This will scare the baby and teach your friend a lesson.

Note: Please search your heart before bringing an infant into your home, as it will tear the family apart with deceit. I have a four-month-old neighbor who is a known cheat.

Restaurant Behavior

So you've decided to treat the family to dinner out. What a terrible idea. Even if you're bringing a bag of emergency clothes, snacks from home, an iPad, iPhone, iTouch, backup Android, markers, stickers, a 1,001-page activity book, and a stuffed bear, you will eventually regret your choice. The only thing toddlers detest more than dinner is dinner in public. There is an enormous amount of pressure to remain seated in restaurants, as well as to maintain lower than reasonable voice-decibel levels. This, combined with the common practice of refusing service to individuals wearing neither shoes nor shirts, is a recipe for disaster.

Everyone knows that toddlers are burrowing animals. Your child will feel most comfortable under the restaurant table. Leave it alone. Public booster seats and high chairs smell like sick and are constricting.

Through my research, I've discovered that the floor directly under the table is spacious, comfortable, and a used-gum factory. Let your child remain out of other diners' sight in order to ensure his happiness.

There is only one course that your toddler is interested in: the bread. Order the fifteen-dollar macaroni and cheese or chicken strips if you must, but understand that you'll be taking it home to feast on at midnight (as if we don't know). Pass your child the breadbasket under the table along with a juice box from home.

Five minutes later, your toddler will be done eating. Your drinks may not have arrived, but now is the time to pack it up and go home. If you decide to stay, know that you are opening yourself up to a world of public embarrassment.

Restaurant behaviors that are perfectly normal but generally distasteful to adults include:

Staring: Like most toddlers, I take extreme delight in making adults feel uncomfortable through my laser beam–like gaze focused directly on a grown-up's face. You'll notice that your child is expressionless as he drills a hole into his target using an intense glare. The joy experienced by your toddler compares to the feeling parents get when five or more people like their Facebook status update.

Loud talking: In order to be heard over the sounds of chatter, clinking plates, and rattling cups, toddlers need to scream anything they'd normally say. There's nothing you can do about this other than tell the entire restaurant to shut their mouths.

Table sweeping: The urge to draw one's arm across the table and make as many items as possible fall to the ground is natural. You should have left already, so blame yourself at this point.

A fifty-cent box of crayons and a menu that doubles as a coloring book are no match for a toddler determined to end a family's evening out. Next time go to the drive-through and eat in the car.

- -
Homework: Go to the drive-through and eat in the car.
- -

Hopefully, now you understand that your child is not a piece of Play-Doh for you to mold or consume. Toddler behaviors are spontaneous, noisy, and sometimes result in broken glass. If you wanted a robot, you should have ordered one online. *Sesame Street* is always saying "Be yourself," and unless you're prepared to call Big Bird a liar, let's go with that.

Popular Toddler Obsessions Explained

Writing on Walls

Every toddler knows what it's like to be persecuted with a time-out for Michelangelo-ing up the walls in his home. It makes me wonder how two-year-old Banksy was received. Probably poorly.

Something else to consider: You claim to love your child's artwork, but only in certain forms—on white computer paper, to be specific. Imagine a world where complex human emotions are expressed only on construction paper. Allow your child's inner artist to develop without limits or consequence. Walls can be Magic Erasered and painted, but a stifled spirit rarely learns how to balance a checkbook.

Peeing Outside

Horses do it. Ants do it. Daddies do it. Peeing outside is how toddlers say, "Life, I like you." If you've ever turned around to see your child peeing against a tree or in a bed of flowers at the park, just pretend you're in a cartoon, and it's not pee but sunshine. Not many adults know this, but toddlers mark their territory, like any other animal. These aromatic cues are how toddlers in the three-and-under network send messages to one another.

Important data is both given and received via pee-pee. Without compromising the confidentiality of the toddler community, the main types of pee-to-nose communications are as follows:

1. **Panic over imminent preschool enrollment/assessment interviews:** Toddlers release an early-warning system to let one another know when it's time to regress and act out to avoid preschool. It's kind of like a tornado warning but with liquid waste. Through different pee profiles, physical descriptions of preschool administrators and interview locations are shared so that toddlers can skillfully sabotage the meeting. One of the many success stories includes two-and-a-half-year-old Tyler, who, when asked his favorite color by his potential preschool teacher, responded with, "Can I lick your arm? People taste good." He did not start school that year.
2. **Jokes:** About 80 percent of all pee communications are viral videos (too complex to explain) and memes.
3. **Toy recall information:** What, you thought you were the only one on top of this?
4. **Politics, tech trends, and science.**

Running in Circles

What you see as meaningless and sporadic movement is actually your toddler attempting time travel. Not many of us succeed, but when we do, it's a thrilling adventure. I've seen dinosaurs close up, and I've been to the future (yes, people can fly but they don't have eyebrows). It works better if your toddler is naked. You won't notice your child being gone, because one earth second equals one time-travel year. No, you can't do it. It's possible only with the head-diameter-to-body-length ratio specific to toddlers.

Parkour

The popularity of this form of street gymnastics has grown significantly within the fitness and attention-seeking communities. What most people don't know is that toddlers invented this activity, but we prefer to just call it "walking." Essentially, it is the act of finding the most life-threatening route from Point A to Point B. Toddler parkour can be done inside or outside as long as the participant is nude. Goggles and hats are fine. Small children know they're doing it right when the blood drains from their caregiver's face. Bonus points if a parent faints. Furniture parkour is a favorite amongst toddlers, so make sure you own at least two sturdy coffee tables, a large couch, and an armchair. Houseplants and throw pillows are natural causalties of this sport.

Note: If you say something like "You're going to hurt yourself," and your toddler does, we're going to assume you willed it to happen.

Dear HT,

I've seen the light and will stop reading crazy parenting books. What should I do with them?

Love you, Reformed Reader

Dear Reformed Reader,

You sound like a smart individual. If you have fire, explode the books in a field. If not, hire a dog to bury them.

xo, HT

2

Parenting from the Heart:
Ignoring Outside Influences

Being a parent is very simple. There is no reason for you to constantly go to other adults who do not know your toddler for advice or conspiring. What happens at home stays at home. Don't be tempted by the latest parenting book from an expert who is not a toddler, and please don't listen to your lying friends. When it comes to being a good parent, the most important resources are the words that come out of your child's amazing mouth. If your child is too young to speak, guess accurately on the first try. In this chapter, we will examine some particularly dangerous influences.

Books

Battle Hymn of the Tiger Mother by some lady

Ah, there's nothing like the smell of a child's freshly broken spirit in the morning. Are. You. Serious.

I was recently made aware of the terrible book *Battle Hymn of the Tiger Mother,* and after I stopped crying, I went to my local library and soaked a copy in grape juice. Then I made sure to consume several of the pages so they'd be processed into something more suitable.

It's easy to spot Tiger Kids at the park. Instead of playing, they're trying to calculate how the angle of the slide will affect the appearance of their overly starched Ralph Lauren jumpers. Who am I kidding, they don't go to the park—their afternoons are spent in tutoring centers. Don't bother sharing your cookies; they have their nightly weigh-in to consider.

Parents who get excited about sucking the fun out of their toddler's life should have adopted a stuffed animal instead of having an actual human baby.

If *Battle Hymn of the Tiger Mother* appeals to you, please carefully fold your toddler's clothes, place them in a sturdy suitcase, and send him off to live with Grandma. Don't bother packing those *Your Baby Can Read!* DVDs, since your kid will be too busy having a—what's the word I'm looking for—CHILDHOOD. Since you'll be relieved of your child-raising duties, feel free to get a new job as a prison guard or an electroshock therapy technician. Use those flash cards to create a papier-mâché child who will never disappoint you.

You're fired.

Bringing Up Bébé by another person

"French kids never cry at the dinner table." Why would they? Have you seen those baguettes? If someone gave me a piece of bread shaped like a sword, I'd be satisfied into a state of silence, too.

Look, I don't have anything against Parisian toddlers, but I need their parents to stop lying. I don't care if your toddler is from Zimbabwe or New Jersey: The kid is going to have loud responses on a regular basis. It's part of toddler/thug life. You're really going to tell me that a child being served pâté (think peanut butter but with animal parts and lard) isn't having a loud response? Riiight. Parents, don't let *Bringing Up Bébé* shame you into thinking there's something wrong with not being refined. Chuck E. Cheese's could be a five-star restaurant if stars were given out based on sticky surfaces. Cloth napkins are as crazy an idea as cloth toilet paper. Some things are meant to be disposable. You don't even need real plates if you're doing the right thing by your family and ordering pizza.

If you're so dedicated to having a calm dinner experience, why did you have children in the first place? Don't try to make your toddler an honorary member of the French Legion just because you can't handle your responsibilities. If you're really dedicated to introducing a little Frenchie into your home, start and end with chocolate croissants.

In conclusion, this book is full of lies because one of my best friends is from Lyon, and she once took a poo-poo under the table during Christmas dinner. Deal with that.

Solve Your Child's Sleep Problems by a fake doctor

Dr. Ferber lives in an abandoned barn in Bakersfield, California, with 106 snakes. One day, as a joke, he decided to write a hilariously crazy book about getting children to sleep through the night by ignoring their basic needs. Unfortunately, the book fell into the wrong hands and was published. Parents around the world who were tired of missing their eight P.M. shows began putting Dr. Ferber's awful ideas into practice.

While the technique is used mostly with infants, you may be tempted to try Dr. Ferber's cry-it-out method on your toddler. Question: Have you ever asked yourself what the "it" being cried out is? It's love. Your child is crying out the love. And while you are standing by the door like a fool, the love is floating out the window.

Children who have been "sleep-trained" grow up to be confused individuals full of problems. Not only will they never eat produce, they won't get any back teeth. Seven out of eight toddlers who have cried it out can't distinguish between an apple and an orange by high school. They are incapable of playing musical instruments.

As we speak, Dr. Ferber is in protective custody due to threats by numerous toddler groups.

Pediatricians

A pediatrician is a doctor who has a hard time knowing where your business begins and theirs ends. Most of these doctors resemble Bruce Willis and have remarkably cold hands. It is common practice for them to ask your child to strip to the diaper and sit on a table lined with parchment paper. Don't try to make sense of it.

Pediatricians will try to fill your head with stories about what's best for your child. Despite what they say, DO NOT ease up on the milk, and DO NOT introduce a reasonable bedtime. If your pediatrician tells you that your toddler needs to eat something other than bread, run out of the room. On your way out, yell "YOU DON'T KNOW OUR LIFE!" and try your best to break something.

Half the time you are in the office, your toddler's doctor will be drawing on a pad of paper, so how seriously can you take her? I love drawing as much as the next person, but if you're going to invite me to your house, at least serve some juice and have snacks ready. Amirite? And if she tries to listen to your child's heartbeat using black magic, things have gone from bad to worse.

Doctors are very curious about the holes of others, specifically the eye, nose, and mouth holes. It's not cute or funny. Pediatricians will ask you to visit often. Leave it up to your toddler.

Most of what a pediatrician does will be harmless, but you need to keep a sharp eye out for vaccines (see what I did with "sharp"?). Vaccines are nothing but stabbings. Usually, your child's doctor will have one of her gang members come in to handle the dirty work. If you fail to stop this assault, consider yourself at best a punk, at worst an accomplice. No Popsicle, dollar-store plastic ring, or sticker is an acceptable apology for your lack of vigilance.

Friends and Family

There are a lot of well-meaning people in your life who will try to give you parenting feedback. Unless they're telling you to build additional shelves in the pantry for fruit snacks, write them off as crazy. Adults love to scheme. Common topics include:

How to get your toddler to sleep through the night no matter who gets hurt.
How to break your toddler's spirit through rules.
How to force your toddler to eat anything because who cares.

The right thing to do when someone you know tries to damage the parent/child relationship is push him in the face. Take your palm and press it against the front of his face, hard. It'll force his neck back and startle him at the same time. The first thing you'll notice is that he'll stop talking. Success! You might think that this is an extreme response, but how far would you go to protect your family? Liam Neeson far? I hope so. Your toddler hopes so, too.

You may love your relatives, but no one is more related to you than your toddler, so make sure you're being loyal to number one. If people who can't keep their terrible ideas to themselves continue bothering your family, consider an electric fence around your home. Invite your friends who think your toddler is too old for the big bed over for cake and juice. When they walk up to the house and get the shock of their lives, stand over them and scream, "THAT'S WHAT HAPPENS."

The next time your best friend at the park starts going on and on about how her wonderful toddler loves mixed greens, don't think about running to the farmers' market. Be stronger than the moment. Just look her in the eye and say, "There are so many lies coming out of your butt right now."

Strangers

People you don't know are always full of ideas about raising a child they've never met. These folks love to chat with parents about what their children are wearing, the length of their hair, and whether or not they should be wearing pants. Even though they're grown-ups and should have a busy agenda full of important tasks, they'll always take the time to make noise pollution with their voices. You don't have to be nice to these individuals. Just say whatever you want.

Below are responses you can use when strangers try to offer unsolicited opinions about your fantastic child.

1. **They say:** Your toddler eats too much junk food.

   You say: *Your breath smells like octopus farts.*

2. **They say:** Why is your toddler running all over the place like a hooligan?

   You say: *Because he loves life. Go drink some weak sauce.*

3. **They say:** Your toddler is making too much noise in the library.

   You say: *Yeah, and he peed near the board books, too. This place is boring. We're out.*

Now you have the tools you need to become an advocate for your child. If it's appropriate, don't hesitate to sweep the leg.

Remember: You and your toddler have a great thing going. People who try to ruin that need to be dealt with severely and swiftly. If you use karate, remember to make a video and share it via You-Tube.

Exemption: Grandparents

Unlike relatives, pediatricians, books, or strangers, you can always count on grandparents to speak the truth about your toddler. In fact, you should learn as much as possible from your child's grandparents, especially when it comes to discipline and snacks. Most grandmas endorse a very gentle no-time-out policy. Like geniuses, they have also elevated cookies and cake from sometime foods to anytime foods. That's called being solution-oriented. Try it out for a change.

I love my parents, but I *love* my grandparents. They know how to treat a person. Your toddler should spend as much time as possible with his grandma and grandpa in order to be loved properly. You've already proved over and over that you have a lot to learn.

Never, I repeat, NEVER poison your toddler's grandparents against him with wild stories you've made up on your own. They're not interested in hearing those and will see right through you.

One of the special skills grandparents have refined is the ability to interpret problem behaviors. Most parents are quick to blame; grandparents, on the other hand, know their grandbabies' hearts. See below for examples.

Angry-Mother Type: My toddler keeps hitting.
Traditional Thoughtless Response: Have you tried a harsh punishment?
Grandma: Your baby is starving. Try doughnuts.

Frustrated Father: My toddler keeps getting out of bed.
Traditional Thoughtless Response: Have you tried a harsh punishment?
Grandpa: Get her a bike.

Overreacting Mom: My toddler keeps breaking precious things.
Traditional Thoughtless Response: Scream "NO" as loud as you can.

Grandma: Your toddler *is* the precious thing. Get your priorities straight.

Furious-for-No-Reason Dad: My toddler is using pee as a weapon.
Traditional Thoughtless Response: Burn all the toys!
Grandpa: LOL

Feel free to call or email your toddler's grandparents anytime you have a question about life. Never assume that you're doing the right thing.

If you humble yourself, there is plenty that you can learn from observing your child's grandparents. Grandmas and grandpas are more refined versions of moms and dads. That may be hard to accept, but there's not much you can do to change it. What you *can* do is open your heart and mind and let the wisdom come in and chase out the foolishness.

Grandmas

Grandmas are moms without all the judgment. You will never hear a grandmother blame her sweet baby for a headache that said child has nothing to do with. Grandmas are not obsessed with potty training and know that it will happen when it happens or not at all. They also realize that naughty behavior is a sign that a child is deficient in the vitamins found specifically in fresh cookies. Ask the grandma in your child's life to teach you about love. Most are willing to give free or low-cost therapy sessions several times a week.

Grandpas

Grandpas are known for their relaxed attitudes. "It's not a big deal" is the mantra of grandfathers, who know that life is not supposed to be a blur of overreactions. If you find yourself yelling, creating arbitrary consequences, or feeling overwhelmed by your child's normal behavior, it's time to call Grandpa and get a new perspective.

The following scenarios illustrate how seeing the world through the eyes of your child's grandma or grandpa will improve your relationship with your child.

As one mom tells it:

It started in the morning. My two-year-old woke up at five A.M., demanding waffles. We were all out of frozen waffles, so I suggested cereal. She screamed no to that and the other five choices available. I tried not to swear. Finally, this child settled down and ate three bites of an apple and two crackers. Getting her dressed proved to be a challenge, as she doesn't see the need for clothes. I was sweating by the time I'd managed to wrestle her little limbs into pants and a T-shirt. I barely turned my back before noticing that she'd removed all of her clothing. I decided to take her to the park to work off some of her energy. She played well for a while but lost it when she saw that the swings were all occupied. I took that as our cue to leave. It's not even lunchtime and I'm exhausted.

The very same morning, from Grandma's perspective:

I arose at four thirty, excitedly anticipating my sweet grandbaby waking up. After I stared at her face for thirty minutes, she finally opened her beautiful eyes and smiled that angelic smile in my direction. We just hugged for several minutes while I recited a poem I wrote for her called "Angel of My Life." I asked her what she wanted for breakfast. Waffles. Only the best for my baby girl, so I prepared a batch from scratch—she even helped stir (gifted)! After a wonderful breakfast, we headed over to the park. She didn't want to wear traditional clothes, so we went in pajamas. I think she's going to be a fashion designer, because she's always thinking outside the box. I have seventeen photos from different angles of the sand castle that this budding architect made. Before leaving, she wanted to go on the swings. Unfortunately, selfish, lesser children were monopolizing them. After I had a quick, stern chat with one of their mothers, my sweetie pie got her turn. Thirty minutes later, we made our way home. This was easily the best day of my life.

Do you see? Is your toddler a problem, or are your eyes? Let's move on to Grandpa vs. Daddy.

Daddy whines:

We took our two-and-a-half-year-old son to a wedding last week. Things started off okay, but getting him to sit still during the ceremony was like trying to shave a monkey. He literally could not contain himself. Right before the bride and groom said their vows, he yelled out, "It smells like farts in here." I was humiliated. The three coloring books, toys, and snacks that we'd brought along were useless. He took no interest in them and instead chose to stare down the guests directly behind us. By the end of the ceremony, I'd fed him almost an entire pack of bribery gum and had no idea where his shoes were. The reception was no better. He rejected the meal entirely and somehow got into the wedding cupcakes before they'd been served. I don't think we'll do this again.

Grandpa's perspective:

Another wedding. The only thing that made it semi-tolerable was my hilarious grandson. During the ceremony, he kept me entertained with some pretty amazing gymnastics. At one point, he shouted, "It smells like farts in here" (it did). I did my best to stifle my laughter. This kid is going places. We found no use for the "activity tote bag" that his parents packed. This boy is way too smart for conventional coloring books. The people behind us provided enough entertainment just by looking weird. By the end of the six-hour ceremony, we'd shared a pack of gum and had both taken off our shoes to get a little more comfortable. The reception was just as fun because of my little guy. The food was terrible, so I promised we'd get pizza afterward. Maestro found where they were keeping the cupcakes and swiped one for each of us. Extremely thoughtful. Fantastic day.

This might be the point where you want to apologize to your toddler for how terrible you've been. Ask the grandparent in your life for schooling in the following areas:

- Calming down
- Coming up with positive reasons for your toddler's "negative" behavior
- Letting things slide
- Relaxing the time-out policy
- Laughing off difficult situations
- Eliminating rules
- Turning sometime foods into anytime foods
- Taking your toddler's requests more seriously
- Seeing the beauty, innocence, brilliance, and genius in your child at every moment
- Reducing angry faces
- Changing your gaze from frustrated to full of wonder
- Not making a big deal

Having dealt with them for quite some time, I know how large the egos of parents are. If you have difficulty bringing yourself to ask your child's grandparent for help, feel free to use the following letter. Just fill in the blanks and mail it out.

Dear _____ [insert name of toddler]'s grandmother and grandfather,

Up until this moment, my listening ears have been closed. I don't know why I'm so full of pride. I mean, for what? What have I done that would make me so proud? For some reason, I have believed that I have it all under control when that couldn't be further from the truth. Bottom line, I've been blaming _____ [insert name of toddler] for a lot of my own problems. Mind doctors call this projecting, and it has been my life's work. I have become an expert in making my young, beautiful, and talented toddler responsible for my emotional outbursts. I have serious problems. I can't let anything go and am constantly making a big deal.

I'm writing to you today because I need help. I see the way you take notice of how amazing, special, unique, and praiseworthy _____ [insert name of toddler] is, and I'd like to see him/her through your eyes.

Are you willing to teach me? I can pay with crash. We can arrange lessons six to seven times a week. Money is no object when it comes to my quest to become a better, less crazy parent. Please let me know if you have time ASAP.

Thank you for considering me as your student, sensei.

Love, _____ [insert your name]

Anatomy of a Grandparent's Hug

Grandparent hugs are mystical. If a grandparent hug were a food, it would be a marshmallow coated in chocolate sauce rolled in cotton candy gently warmed by unicorn breath. Science has shown that these hugs have the power to heal boo-boos in the absence of Band-Aids. Parents, learning to hug like a grandparent is a five-step process that requires dedication. If you're up for it and able to master the art, you'll have a very happy toddler.

1. Clear your head of any to-dos. You have nowhere to be.
2. Believe that your toddler is a perfect being devoid of character flaws.
3. Don't go in for the hug. Lower your body to crouch level and outstretch your arms. Smile like it's Christmas.
4. Your toddler will be drawn to your magnetic field. Allow your excitement to grow.
5. You're now in full embrace. Nuzzle close and take deep breaths of your toddler's hair while you gently squeeze and cuddle her small form.

Grandparents and New Babies

Everyone has flaws, and sadly, grandparents are not exempt. The kryptonite to the grandparent/toddler relationship is a new baby. When new babies come into a home, they believe it is their right to share everything: air, mothers, fathers, and yes, grandparents. If you're thinking, "They have no right," you are on the right track. Grandparents, if you're reading this, do not get sucked in by the smell of fresh baby.

Sometimes the remix of a song can be interesting, but it will never hold a candle to the original. "There's enough love to go around." Grandma, this isn't true. If you want your number one toddler to have a full cup, you need to save all of your love for him. There's nothing worse for a toddler than seeing his grandparents hold another child. Don't get into the habit.

If a new infant arrives, you don't have to be rude to it, but keep a safe distance. Avoid looking the baby in the eye, especially if your toddler is present. When your grandchild's mom and dad talk about the infant, hum loudly.

You're now equipped to deal with an infant apocalypse. Don't think it can't happen to you.

Popular Toddler/Grandparent Activities

The types of activities your toddler engages in with his grandparents are not always parent-sanctioned. That said, please keep the judgments to yourself. Popular toddler-approved activities with grandparents include:

1. **Visits to quick-food restaurants.** I've purposely avoided saying "fast food," as the term carries a negative connotation. French fries are a vegetable born of Mother Nature. Try to remember that the next time your toddler comes back from lunch with Grandpa smelling like canola oil.

2. **Toy-store spree.** "My toddler has enough toys." Is that right? According to whom, may I ask? Jealousy is a dangerous emotion. You'll know when your toddler has enough toys when . . . Just kidding, such a state doesn't exist on earth.

3. **Toddler parade.** This is when grandparents drive a toddler all over town, showing him off to their friends. A baked and, preferably, frosted treat is served at every stop.

4. **Impulse day.** When was the last time you asked your toddler what she would like to do and followed through? If you're a grandparent, it was last week. These outings will be mad dashes from the zoo to the movie theater to the play center to the ice-cream parlor and topped off with some pizza. If your toddler collapses or throws up upon his return home, you'll know it's been a good day.

I conducted brief interviews with each of my parents, Grandma, and Grandpa to give you a sense of the main issues facing toddlers today. While our discussions didn't go exactly as planned, I feel they provide valuable insight.

Interview with Mama

Me: What exactly is your problem?

Mama: I don't have a problem, but you need to watch your tone. You smell like poo. Did you poo?

Me: Snacks. Do we have any?

Mama: You just ate. Did you put my cell-phone charger somewhere?

Me: It's in a safe place, try to forget about it. Snacks. Roll them out.

Mama: No.

[*short intermission*]

Me: Thank you for rejoining me.

Mama: You helped yourself to peanut butter?

Me: No . . . why do you ask?

Mama: Your hand is still in the jar.

[*I was running late for another appointment and abruptly had to end the interview here.*]

Interview with Grandma

Me: Hi, Grammy Grams.

Grandma: I love you, sweet baby.

Me: I love you, too.

Grandma: You look so skinny. Are they feeding you?

Me: No, they're not.

Grandma: My poor angel.

Me: I know.

Grandma: Do you need cookies?

Me: Yes, Grammy.

Grandma: What kind would you like me to make, darling?

Me: [*smiling*]

Grandma: Chocolate chip?

Me: You know me so well, Gram-Grams. Come over anytime, we'll be here. Not at the park.

Grandma: My poor angel.

Me: I know.

Grandma: Do you have any toys?

Me: None worth mentioning, why?

Grandma: Because I bought you a bag of them!

Me: No way! I don't deserve those!

Grandma: Who told you that?

Me: Guess.

Grandma: [*shaking her head*]

Interview with Daddy

Me: Hi, Daddy!

Daddy: Please tell me where my wallet is.

Me: [*laughing*]

Daddy: Where did you put it?

Me: How tall are you?

Daddy: I need to know.

Me: Are you part giant?

Daddy: This isn't funny.

Me: You have so much hair on your body. How does that make you feel?

Daddy: I'm going to give you one more chance.

Me: Or what?

Daddy: [*staring at me*]

Me: Juice, please.

Daddy: We have water.

Me: Fascinating. Juice, please.

Daddy: Would you like some water?

Me: JUICE, PLEASE.

Daddy: You can have some water.

[*I think I blacked out at this point—can't remember.*]

Interview with Grandpa

Me: Hello, Grandpa.

Grandpa: Hey there, scamp! What's on your face? Have you been eating lotion?

Me: Yes. Were you born before fire existed? How old are you?

Grandpa: Older than you can count. Where are your clothes?

Me: I took them off.

Grandpa: That's one way to live.

Me: I got in trouble today.

Grandpa: What happened?

Me: I have no idea.

Grandpa: It's usually like that.

[*Then he pulled a dollar out of my ear and we shared a box of Thin Mints.*]

The tone of the interviews is what I'd like you to notice. Make it your new goal to love not like a parent but like a grandparent.

- -

Homework: Keep a journal of your transformation from parent to grandparent. If you haven't improved within six weeks of serious study, have Grandma and Grandpa move in.

- -

Dear Honest Toddler,

My two-year-old begs for scraps when I'm making dinner but seems to be disgusted by the actual meal once it has been completed. What's the problem?

—Scratching My Head in Maine

Dear Scratching,

Your recipes.

Warmly, HT

3

Toddler-Approved Recipes

Toddlers should eat whatever is placed in front of them. Psych! I know you think you know how to make food. Judging by the fact that you think figs are edible, this isn't true. Please pay close attention to this chapter, as your child is probably suffering as we speak.

Toddler Nutrition

Do not go to the Internet for information on feeding your toddler. It's full of lies and blog posts. Toddlers need to eat from the following five food groups daily:

RED: Popsicles, certain apples, and juice all fit into the red category. Be sure that toddlers enjoy some red each and every day.

WHITE: Normal bread, birthday cake, pasta without seasoning, pizza, and marshmallows are all part of a healthy white diet. Don't make a big deal.

JUICE: Better than water, this liquid will help your toddler advance in life. Resist the urge to get weird about it.

CHEESE: If you see a cheese on the Food Network, it's the wrong kind. Only two types of cheese are toddler-appropriate: yellow and string.

CHOCOLATE: Be generous.

Increase the love and respect in your family by making sure your toddler eats a well-balanced red, white, juice, cheese, and chocolate diet. If, for some reason, your toddler wants to go for days eating from only one group or not at all (milk fast), leave it alone.

Breakfast

Whether your toddler wakes up furious or happy, she will need something to eat while watching television. Here is a chance to prove that you are teachable. Breakfast is the most important meal of the day, yet three in five toddlers find themselves faced with sadness in a bowl (oatmeal). Be somebody great today and choose one of the recipes provided.

Toast with Butter

Hold on to your seat! This is a yummy one!

Step 1: Find an unbroken piece of perfect bread with no rips.

Step 2: Put in toaster. Don't get distracted by a Facebook fight that you have no business participating in.

Step 3: When toast pops out, INSPECT IT. Is it a uniform golden-brown color? Is it still intact? If not, return to Step 1.

Step 4: Butter toast liberally. Almond butter is not butter. Don't get cute.

Step 5: Ask toddler how she would like toast cut. Don't make assumptions. You don't know anything about anything.

Step 6: Serve toast.

Step 7: Has toddler changed his mind about toast? Does toddler want cut-up toast to be whole again? Repair toast with your mind.

If you're not powerful enough, return to Step 1 AS MANY TIMES AS IT TAKES. DON'T BE LAZY.

Cereal

Step 1: Find a good cereal. Good cereals have pieces that are all the same (i.e., not granola). If you are a wonderful parent, you own a cereal like Corn Pops. Reach for the stars and get Froot Loops.

Step 2: Put cereal in a toddler-approved bowl. Before pouring, ask toddler if bowl is okay.

Step 3: Ask toddler if he would like milk.

Step 4: Pour milk (optional).

Step 5: Serve cereal.

Step 6: After toddler has eaten one to two bites, throw away cereal without sighing or having a bad attitude.

Step 7: Pour one cup of dry cereal into Ziploc bag.

Step 8: Give to toddler to eat around the house and in front of shows.

Oatmeal

I didn't want to write about this form of hot cereal because it hurts me so, but if my words can save just one toddler from a morning of crying into her pajama sleeve, so be it. Oatmeal is made from rat's milk and bread crusts. The dish was almost extinct when Pinterest made it popular again by serving it in mason jars. You can easily identify toddlers who eat oatmeal on a regular basis by their glassy eyes.

Pasta

Tossed with clam sauce and sun-dried tomatoes. Smothered with creamy Alfredo sauce with seared scallops. There are so many ways to ruin pasta. If you've been given the honor of a feeding a toddler, turn off your cell phone and take it seriously.

Below are a few pasta recipes to cut out and save.

Spaghetti

Step 1: Get a box or bag of normal spaghetti. Make sure it isn't whole wheat (i.e., full of gravel and dust).

Step 2: Cook the pasta with steam until it is soft. Al dente is for adults trying to impress their peers. Just cook it all the way and stop trying to be somebody you're not.

Step 3: Melt all the butter in your home and pour it on top.

Step 4: Look over at the cupboard. Your toddler has already pushed a chair up to the counter and is selecting a bowl.

Step 5: Clean up any broken pieces from dropped dishes without making a big deal.

Step 6: Serve pasta with a fruit juice. Not a vegetable/fruit juice blend. Buy deceptive juices only if you're willing to mix tomato juice with your nightly wine. Don't be a hypocrite.

Spinach-Stuffed Ravioli

Step 1: NOPE.

Lasagna

Lasagna is actually quite delicious when properly prepared. Follow the directions below, and this Italian classic will quickly become a family favorite!

Step 1: Pick up a ready-made lasagna from the grocery store.

Step 2: Allow lasagna to defrost completely on the counter.

Step 3: Scoop lasagna out of aluminum dish and gently place in the trash.

Step 4: Scrub dish until it is free of lasagna debris.

Step 5: Remove box of cake mix from the pantry.

Step 6: Prepare cake mix as directed on the box. Don't forget to let your sweet baby lick the spoon!

Step 7: Pour cake mix into the clean lasagna pan.

Step 8: Place lasagna in the oven.

Step 9: When cooked through, frost lasagna and serve to your happy family. You've done a great thing.

Pesto Pasta

I don't have much to say about this. Seems to me that you think you're the next Jamie Oliver. If you're insistent on cooking Pesto Pasta so you can take Instagram photos with the caption "Yum," make the following modifications so your toddler doesn't become dehydrated from crying.

Step 1: Buy some pesto. You'll find it in the "Tears" section of the grocery store.

Step 2: Open the package and take in the sharp smell, reminiscent of sippy-cup cheese.

Step 3: Like a fool, spread pesto everywhere.

Step 4: Show your toddler what happened.

Step 5: Pick your toddler up off the floor and just hold her for a few minutes while she sobs.

Step 6: Using a mild soap, wash that dirty pasta clean.

Step 7: Notice that your toddler still hasn't forgiven you.

Step 8: Order cheese pizza.

The moral of this tale is to keep that ego in check.

Salad

Salad breaks hearts on a daily basis. Contrary to popular belief, it's not even a real food. If it's not okay to eat leaves at the park, it's not okay to put a salad in front of an innocent. If you want to learn more about how salad destroys families, look at America.

Caesar Salad

Caesar was a very lonely man based out of West Virginia. One day he fell off a bridge. While he was unconscious, a witch tapped him on the head and, through the powers of inception, gave him a salad recipe that included not only raw eggs but anchovies. If someone you love tries to feed your toddler a Caesar salad, remove him or her from your life.

Cobb Salad

If you want bacon, just ask for it. Don't hide it in lettuce. Bacon is delicious and a toddler-approved food. Cobb salad is a no-no food because it promotes waste and shame.

Spinach Salad

The first time I heard of this particular salad, I thought it was a joke and started laughing. My laughter quickly turned to screams. Studies have shown that toddlers who are asked to eat spinach salad develop feelings of distrust toward their guardians.

Tuna Salad

Is it safe to say you no longer care? Why are you doing this? Never serve tuna salad to a toddler unless what you mean to say is: "Hey there, tiny person, you mean very little to me." Four out of five toddlers who consume tuna salad cannot find work as adults.

Fruit

Fruit tastes good and is good for you. My favorite fruits are apples, bananas, red Popsicles, blueberries, and pudding.

Parents, before you hand someone you love a piece of fruit, inspect it. Ask yourself:

1) Does this fruit look like it was grown in an enchanted orchard or under a freeway?
2) Does this fruit look like it has come into direct contact with a rare strain of jungle bacteria causing discoloration or unexplained spots/bumps?
3) Is this fruit small enough to be held comfortably in a toddler-sized hand, or is it one million pounds?
4) Is this fruit wet?

Once fruit has passed its initial inspection, please move on to the subset of criteria.

Apples

Use your X-ray vision to determine if the apple will have brown spots inside. Apples with inside sicknesses can be fed to goats and horses but not children. Being remarkably cheap (don't use words like "frugal" to describe your neurosis) and attempting to remove the disgusting with a knife is unacceptable. Did this apple not cost twenty cents? This should go without saying, but the ENTIRE piece of fruit has been compromised.

Bananas

Bananas are a tricky bunch.

One minute you need a banana. Crave one. Feel like your life won't be the same if you can't enjoy the smooth sweetness of this tropical fruit. So often, though, by the time an adult has gotten off Facebook and peeled one for you, the feeling has passed. This isn't your toddler's fault. Don't make a big deal. Just freeze the banana for a smoothie you will never make, or eat it yourself.

In the future, triple-confirm with your toddler that it is okay for you to peel the banana. When given the green light, peel the banana only one-third of the way down so it doesn't break in half and fall on the floor. Why should I even have to say that?

If there are rotten patches on the banana, do not hand to your toddler with rot patch facing away, like a sneak. Find another banana. If there are no more bananas, OMG.

Buy only bananas without strings on the inside. Read the label.

Toddlers are small people with small stomachs. Usually one to one and a half bites are enough. If your toddler is preparing for battle, two to three whole bananas will be consumed rapidly. Again, don't make a big deal.

Berries

Wash, dry, and make sure they're all uniform. Berries are supposed to be sweet, so if you got a bad batch, shame on you.

Pudding

This fruit comes in small containers and should always be chocolate. Serve with toddler's favorite spoon. Always have more, 'cause you can't eat just one.

Red Popsicles

Not to be confused with yellow or orange Popsicles and definitely not purple Popsicles, these fruits are undeniably delicious. Keep them in the freezer and don't be stingy. Fruit makes a wonderful breakfast, and red Popsicles are no exception. They taste best when enjoyed in front of the TV. No napkin.

Preparation

Sometimes fruit is great cut up. Sometimes cutting removes the flavor. Just ASK.

Now you know how to prepare fruit. Try it today!

Sidenote: Do not remove stickers before serving. If the fruit is not for you, the sticker isn't, either. Greed.

Vegetables

Ninety-nine percent of vegetables are not fit for human consumption. The other 1 percent is ketchup.

Adults, it's time for you to admit that you hate eating vegetables as much as children do. We see the way you slather them in bacon bits, creamy dressings, and cheese just to get them down. Even after they're masked, you still eat salad at an alarming speed to prevent yourself from realizing what's happening. Be honest: Vegetables make you angry.

Most people aren't aware of the backstory behind popular veggies. See below. You're welcome in advance.

Artichokes: Perfectly named, these desert "flowers" will stop up your throat in a hurry. They are eaten by scraping bits of plant off a hard green tusk with your top teeth (you can't make this stuff up). Grown-ups think they like them dipped in butter. Foolishness—what isn't delicious dipped in butter? If you're going to make a condiment do all of the heavy lifting in a recipe, at least give it due credit. You know you hate artichokes.

Asparagus: These small diseased trees are nature's original scarecrows.

Broccoli: Broccoli is a strain of antibiotic-resistant swamp moss. In its hardened form, it's often served alongside heartbreaking entrées such as pork chops and meat loaf. Most toddlers would rather induce vomiting than choke down a single floret. Broccoli is a gateway drug to cauliflower.

Carrots: Carrots seem harmless and are a popular vehicle for ranch dressing. Keep in mind that 85 percent of people who eat carrots forget their own names within twenty-four hours.

Celery: Mmmm, food with indigestible strings. Eat celery if you enjoy sobbing, because that's what you'll be doing after one of its fibrous ropes attacks your gums. Good luck with your life.

Eggplant: This vegetable starts telling lies right off the bat; it does not come from eggs and therefore cannot take part in a breakfast sandwich. Eggplant stole its look from bowling pins. It tastes like frustration.

Onions: Every thirty seconds, a toddler faints due to onion violence. Even adults cry when exposed.

Peas: Unlike popcorn, in the case of this vegetable, you CAN eat just one. Requiring your toddler to eat a bowl of peas fresh out of the microwave is negligent parenting, and you deserve whatever happens to you.

Zucchini: Once cooked, zucchini takes on the texture of bread soaked in chicken broth. If you put this "food" in front of your toddler, expect to be named as the defendant in a future lawsuit.

Parents, don't believe the hype. There is nothing especially nutritious about vegetables. You eat them all the time, yet you're always exhausted, no? Toddlers barely eat vegetables and have boundless energy, so let the evidence speak for itself.

Five-Minute Snacks

Not all meals need to be big productions. In fact, the best ones take only a few minutes and can be made without a trip to the market. Don't believe me? You never do.

Organic Baked Chicken Rounds with Potato Spears

This recipe will take under five minutes, but only if you're already in the drive-through.

Step 1: After the voice prompt, order organic baked chicken rounds with potato spears. They might also be called chicken nuggets and fries, depending on your region, but it's the same thing.

Step 2: Enjoy your meal in the car. Put on some music to create whatever mood you'd like.

Deconstructed Bruschetta Bites

Unlike regular bruschetta, which tastes like pizza's ugly cousin, these healthy finger foods can go from lunch to dinner with a couple of simple modifications.

Step 1: Cut circles out of white bread with cookie cutters.
Step 2: Place a piece of string cheese next to the bread.
Step 3: Dice up a Roma tomato.
Step 4: Serve your toddler the bread and cheese. Eat the tomato when you're alone, because nobody wants to see that.
Dinner version: Add a glass of strawberry or chocolate milk for important protein.

Peanut-Butter Bites with Kale

Step 1: Open a jar of peanut butter.
Step 2: Insert spoon.
Step 3: Eat peanut butter from spoon while shouting "Kale!" a few times.

Healthy Green Smoothie

Step 1: Mix blueberries, strawberries, fresh spinach, almond milk, and walnut oil in a large blender.
Step 2: Pour the drink into a toddler cup with straw.
Step 3: Serve to a stranger child who has offended you recently.

Multicolored Salad

Step 1: Empty economy-sized bag of Skittles into a bowl.
Step 2: Taste the rainbow.

Gum

You may not know this, but gum is a breakfast food. Relax your mind and accept that. Gum comes in two flavors: fruit and minty. It pairs wonderfully with cheese, and on a rainy day, it'll warm your toddler from the inside out.

When you share your gum, you're modeling good behavior. When you hoard it like a criminal, you hurt everyone around you. The worst thing you can do when trying to establish positive relations with your toddler is to lie and say you don't have gum while your breath smells like a peppermint explosion. Who do you think you're fooling? Any gum you have needs to be split 50/50. If you have an eight-pack, that's seven for your toddler and one for your toddler later on. Learn your math.

To raise the happiest toddler on the block, pick up a Costco-sized box of gum on the first Monday of each month. Open it and leave the box in your toddler's room for him to eat as he pleases. Make snow angels in the wrappers.

Yogurt/Lotion

The only difference between yogurt and lotion is the container. They both smell and taste great. Lotion/yogurt is full of calcium and essential for building strong bones. Encourage your toddler to eat yogurt/lotion naked so that the body can be nourished both inside and out. If the mess bothers you, think of why you became a parent and get your head straight.

Cake

Cake is nature's vitamin. Enjoy it on its own or with some cookie dough. Respected scientists say toddlers should have at least three servings of cake daily in order to remember their letters. If you want to raise a dunce, go easy on it. If an idiot is what you want, serve it only on birthdays.

Cake comes in two colors: chocolate and white. German chocolate cake is when fools add coconut. Do you want to be a fool? It's a simple question. Adding vegetable or fruit puree to a cake changes it into trash. The wonderful thing about cake is that it is simple to make, and the ingredients are usually on hand if they aren't being wasted in omelets.

I'll leave you with an Albert Einstein quote: "Make every day a celebration. Bake a cake." He was a good man.

Note: Broken Food

Even though the grocery store is bursting with options, one of the main toddler complaints I hear has to do with broken food. Adults, you don't look cute or smart when you hand your child broken anything. You come off as rude and disrespectful.

Yesterday I was handed one-third of a granola bar, and several lights went out in my head. I cried on and off for thirty minutes. Today is for healing. It is common knowledge that eating broken food leads to a rapid loss of life force, not to mention it tastes different/awful. The molecules in, say, a heart-healthy chocolate-chip cookie are designed to be consumed in round form. When you serve it in a broken half-moon, the elementary particles hurt your toddler's brain and feelings. Do you want that to happen, or do you strive to be a loving person?

Maybe it will help to think about why you decided to become a parent. Most likely, you were bored and looking for someone to serve. Now that you have the opportunity to make your life mean something, do your best. Wake up with a smile on your face and say this fourteen times: "Broken food is disgusting. When I serve it, I look a little ugly."

Those of you who operate cracker factories have the responsibility to innovate until you develop packaging that can preserve the integrity of each individual cracker. Half the product in those boxes has to be thrown out due to chipped edges and premature crumbification. Especially Ritz, which are apparently made with air vapor and therefore cannot be enjoyed in a Ziploc bag for long before converting into stovetop stuffing mix.

I find it very curious that bottles of wine are always stored impeccably. When it comes to beverages, you adults seem to know just what to do.

Crackers aren't the only foods that are prone to breakage. Pieces of fruit, bread, even rice can be too broken for consumption. Broken rice is called couscous in some circles and will devastate your family. Please go ahead and serve it if you don't care about anyone but yourself. That's fine.

Trying to manually put a crust corner back on a piece of toast or conceal brokenness in other poorly thought-out ways is embarrassing for both parties.

You might be asking yourself, "What can I do with all of this broken food?" You have two simple options: Either eat it in private, or throw it away. Just because your toddler may or may not have eaten trash in the past doesn't mean he or she is an actual trash can.

The next time your toddler expresses a bit of upset over being handed something broken, stifle your laughter, calm your tantrum, and be professional. Customer service isn't for everyone, but if you maintain a teachable spirit, you should be fine.

Juice

Recently, special-interest groups have launched a smear campaign against juice. Full-strength juice is as nutritious as it is delicious. Unless you plan on watering down your pinot noir, don't you dare serve your toddler intentionally weakened fruit beverages. Ruining perfectly good juice by cutting it with lukewarm tap water is disrespectful and shows that you know nothing about friendship.

The best way to present your toddler with juice is in small boxes. Individual containers are sold in grocery stores next to the chips that you never seem to have enough money for. Keep the house stocked. Act like other people in the family are important. There is no need to place arbitrary limits on how much juice your toddler can consume on a daily basis. The human body is 75 percent juice, so it has to be right.

A very popular form of juice, soda, has also been shown to help toddlers think.

Vitamins

If you're eating all of your toddler's gummy vitamins late at night, consider yourself a failure. Are you that hungry? What a shame.

Side Dishes

Every single day, thousands of toddlers contact me concerning their problems with side dishes. Mashed potatoes with chives, stuffed mushroom caps . . . I can barely write this without getting noticeably upset. Parents, I understand your commitment to side dishes, so I have created a simple list of heart-healthy alternatives.

Happy Toddler Side Dishes
- Peanut butter
- Rice Krispies Treats
- Jelly beans
- Red rope/Red Vines
- Fruit snacks
- Mandarin orange slices in the plastic container, packed in juice, not water
- Lucky Charms (just the marshmallows)
- Small toys or gifts

- Play-Doh
- Crayons
- Playing outside

At this time, I'd like to admit that I have forgotten the purpose of this list. I'm sorry.

Popcorn

YES.

Butternut Squash

No.

Brown Rice

Brown rice is what happens when you give up on a dream. This food looks and tastes like a rough draft. DO NOT serve brown rice to your toddler under any circumstances. The people who invented brown rice are in hiding and did not respond to my interview requests.

Lentils

Lentils taste like wartime and look like destruction. They're the perfect punishment for a traitor.

Kombucha

You clearly have more money than you know what to do with if you're buying kombucha. Take some of that cash and start a college fund, because we know your child doesn't have one. Fermented liquid can be found for free under car seats and behind couches.

Playdate Food

Lucky you! You're having toddlers over for some fun. When you're done hiding the dirty dishes and piles of laundry, consider your food situation. Peer pressure from other parents might confuse you into thinking that carrot sticks and celery are a good idea, but you're dead wrong. Making baby Caprese salads or picking up some baklava to impress other moms and dads means you're as weak as a duckling.

DO NOT try to make something that you can easily buy at the store. From scratch Cheez-Its? You serious? Scrap together four dollars and treat the kids to a box of the real thing. Homemade fruit leather looks like placenta. Get some Fruit Roll-Ups and call it a day.

Unless you're the queen of England, do not serve tea. Soda or juice. Nobody traveled that far for water, either. Increase your child's popularity by offering your guests Halloween candy or s'mores.

Seasonings, Spices, and Sauces

Seasonings, spices, and sauces have one thing in common: They're the devil's work. Spices are acorn shavings and dirt specks that many parents add to a finished meal in order to test a toddler's patience. Stop. There is a time and place for eating dirt, and that's not your call. Most sauces taste like hot snot. If you're tempted to pour a melted food over a regular food, take three giant steps back from the stove and make a life change. Ask yourself why right after you order some white rice.

Dinner Service

While it is customary in many countries to eat sitting around a table, most toddlers feel that hurts their life force. Philosophers recommend abandoning traditional and stifling mealtimes in favor of the more sophisticated "cattle grazing" approach. This method is very simple to implement in your home. All it takes is a willing spirit. Your willing spirit. Your toddler can carry on as is.

A Beginner's Guide to Implementing Toddler Grazing

Step 1: Relax your forehead.

Step 2: Accept that your ideas are wrong.

Step 3: Forget yourself.

Step 4: Throw away your plates.

Step 5: In every room of the house, even the bathroom, erect a small table.

Step 6: On each table, place two pieces of buttered toast, a generous bowl of M&M's, a small bag of cereal, four juice boxes, ten string cheeses, and a Go-Gurt.

Step 7: Allow your toddler to eat as she pleases while moving through the house. Replenish the food supply as necessary.

Step 8: Pat yourself ONCE on the back.

Most of your toddler's food problems have been caused by poor parenting. Rather than dwell on your feelings of shame, get inspired to make a change. If you followed your instincts, you'd know that foods like soup and casserole are not even real. When you feel like being inventive, step out of the kitchen. Ask nicely, and I will allow you to borrow some paper and a few crayons.

It is common for adults to let their terrible ideas get in the way of being good people. Now you have the tools. The rest is up to you. *Bon appétit.*

4

Food-Shopping Guide:
What We DO and DON'T Need

Grocery shopping can be a wonderful experience that brings your family closer together, or it can be the worst thing that has happened to your toddler since the placenta. The choice is yours, really. So before you grab those reusable shopping bags for the sake of the earth, consider the child, who is, after all, your whole universe.

Timing

You've seen what happens when you visit the park at three P.M.: Every Dick and Sally is there with pails and shovels. Infants are monopolizing the swings and sitting like fools at the bottom of the slide. The same goes for grocery-store trips. Peak hours need to be avoided for the comfort of your young one.

Between the hours of four and six, you need to skip shopping for food unless you've always been curious about how it feels to be inside an operating food processor. With all those people around and stranger danger at record highs, the chances of your toddler being able to roam freely without shoes in the late afternoon are slim. Grocery-store floors are perfect for running at high speeds.

They're polished but not slick. It's like walking on the moon. Don't waste the opportunity.

Do not go to the other extreme and show up at the store at nine A.M. sharp. Boxes are still being unloaded, and this type of industrial debris will prevent your child from achieving Mach speeds. You may not have goals right now, but your child does, and most of them center on being as fast as possible. Toddler self-esteem is directly linked to how quickly one's legs rotate.

Grocery-Store Layout

After doing minutes of research at a grocery outlet in my area, I have included a detailed guide to help expedite your shopping experience.

Not all sections of the grocery store are created equal. It's easy for parents to get confused and start putting all kinds of items that nobody enjoys in the cart. No matter how many times the bagged salad goes bad and is thrown away unopened, adults continue to live in denial. Following this guide will save you millions.

Doors

Use them to go in and out. If there is an available cart near the entrance, take one, but accept that your toddler may or may not want to sit in it. That is her decision and her decision alone. Most toddlers prefer to walk directly in front of the cart or run several miles ahead of it.

Garden

This is where farmers throw the fruits and vegetables they don't know what to do with. Pick up a bunch of perfect grapes and four apples with no blemishes. If you are tempted by the radishes, pray until the feeling passes. You'll see vegetables that don't exist in nature; just keep walking and try not to look. As I stated above,

no one in your family will eat salad, so just stop. Get some tanger-
ines but only if they're peeled. Asparagus is not real. Two-thirds of
these fruits and vegetables are for decoration only.

Milk

This area is located in the back of the grocery store. All of the
items come from the underside of a cow. Don't let that bother you,
as it's donated, not stolen. Pick up a hundred yogurts. Look for
designs from TV on the label. Individually wrapped small cups are
ideal. Skip the yogurt with fruit on the bottom—if a company can't
take the time to stir, what other corners are they cutting? Get all
the string cheese. Buy some milk for the days when your toddler
doesn't feel like eating solid foods.

Rows and Rows

These aisles are a mixed bag. You need to put on your thinking cap
and stay alert. Baked goods are an obvious yes, as are juice, crackers, cereal, white rice (sometimes), and marshmallows. Even if you
have money to burn, your toddler will get acid reflux on the spot if
you so much as pick up a can of garbanzo beans packed in water.
Being a grown-up is a big responsibility. Don't abuse your powers
by buying flaxseed. At this point, your toddler will be running, so
you don't have time to fool around with canned salmon and capers
anyway.

Arctic Zone

Grab a warm hoodie, because this is by far the craziest part of the
grocery store. You'll barely believe your eyes, but it's right there in
front of you: ice cream chilling next to mixed vegetables. This is
to throw you off. It's the final test. Whether or not you will make
the right decision is a reflection of your character. Open the glass
door, select ice cream with no nuts, and put it inside your cart. That
wasn't hard. Popsicles are fruit excess in cold form, so get a box. If

you spot frozen chicken nuggets and corn dogs, grab them for an easy and nutritious everyday meal solution.

You're almost out of the grocery store! Congrats!

Candyland

As a final thank-you from the store, the payment area will be lined with delicious treats to ensure a happy send-off. Take whatever you want. Your toddler most surely has! It's like trick-or-treat but day-time.

How does it feel to have made the first successful shopping trip in your career as a parent? On the way home, pick up some food at a drive-through, as it's best to let groceries rest for a full twenty-four hours.

Stealing vs. Sampling

Grocery stores often give out samples of their foods to encourage you to keep up your energy levels while shopping. This makes perfect sense, and there's nothing wrong with it. Similarly, your toddler may open up a bag of Cheetos while your back is turned. It's the same concept; one just requires initiative and courage. Children know when their blood sugar is low, and if your angel decides to take matters into his own hands, the only suitable response is a high five.

Adults, there's no reason to be shy about consuming food in a grocery store. That's like being ashamed of singing in a music store or jumping on a bed at IKEA: It's what you're there to do. The next time your toddler opens a pack of rice crackers with her teeth, don't make a big deal. If it bothers you, look the other way.

The good thing about eating while you shop is that anything you consume on-site in a grocery store is free. Visit on an empty stomach, and you'll save thousands of dollars a year. If your toddler puts a small candy in her pocket, don't bust her, because that could very well be a gift for you. Help your little gifter make her way out the front door undetected. Look at you working as a family!

Dangerous and Shady Individuals

The grocery store is full of people you need to be aware of for the safety of your toddler. If you know what to look for, staying protected will be easy. Keep an eye on:

1. **Infants and small babies:** These people have no respect for the bond between other children and their parents. They will do everything and anything to get your attention. If you see one in a stroller, don't spend a lot of time looking at it and wishing your toddler were that small. There's nothing special about babies, and half of them are pickpockets, so don't get too close. If you ask a baby's caregiver how old it is, your toddler will move out the next day. Keep your attention focused on the child you came to the store with.

2. **Behaving toddlers:** Seeing another toddler sitting quietly in his cart reading a newspaper will make you think there is something wrong with your child. Don't compare, because that child is probably sick. You don't know anything about him. He could be a spy. Pointing at this dummy while saying to your child, "Why can't you act like that?" is Level 10 wrong. If you want that kid so much, why don't you trade? Because you can't, so get over it.

3. **Strangers:** Every once in a while, a person will come over and attempt to pat your toddler on the head: "Aren't you cute?" Unless your toddler is not a real person and actually is a show dog, get between this stranger and the light of your life. Use your body as a shield. Don't punk out. You're the only thing between the threat and your child's well-being. Unless it is obvious that the individual has candy she'd like to distribute, don't hesitate to engage in full-scale combat.

4. **Store employees:** Even though these people are supposed to just clean up the milk your toddler spilled, they often overstep their role. Nobody needs to tell your toddler to remain seated in the cart or not to remove price stickers. If someone who works at the grocery store tries to invoke martial law, ask him to come back with a warrant. No judge alive will grant one, so don't worry. Managers in particular like to go on and on about where people can use the bathroom and where they can't. If a control-freak manager gets in your face, take down his badge number and file a formal complaint with the precinct.

In-Store Communication

How you speak to your toddler can make the difference between terrible memories of food shopping or great ones for her to share with her psychologist. Below are the most common and hurtful phrases parents say to their sunshine while in grocery stores. Avoid them unless you want to appear as the antagonist in your baby's future memoirs.

"Don't touch that."

Are we in a museum? Walking through ancient ruins? Taking a tour through the Pentagon? This is a grocery store, not a house of cards. Your toddler will not be the first one to break a dozen or so eggs. The cleanup crew knows just what to do.

"Walk, don't run."

Breathe, don't sneeze. Pump your blood slower. Make clouds with your hands. Do you see how crazy impossible requests sound?

"We can't afford that."

Really. You can't break a twenty for a Cadbury egg. We're honestly supposed to believe that a product under five dollars is out of the budget when a bottle of wine, twelve-dollar organic honey, and two bars of dark chocolate are sitting in the cart? On what island are those considered life necessities?

"That's not good for you."

Again, I'd like to call in to evidence the wine and dark chocolate.

"I'll think about it"/"We'll see."

Of all the lies parents tell, the worst leave a hope residue. Don't do that. Everyone within earshot knows you have no intention whatsoever of purchasing those Double Stuf Oreos.

"We're almost done."

How can that be the case when you seem determined to read the story on the side of every single box? Toddlers enjoy good books as much as the next person, but we have the decency to read them at home. Not every step of life has to be entertaining.

"Take only one."

Come again?

It's funny. So many parents know how to talk but not *how* to talk. A knowledge bomb has just exploded in your face. You can duck for cover or let the shrapnel fill you with wisdom.

Anatomy of a Grocery-Store Meltdown

So you've done everything right, but your toddler is still lying facedown on the linoleum, crying. Your face is hot with embarrassment and frustration as judgy strangers shoot you scathing reviews of your parenting. The good news is: Your toddler isn't repressing his feelings. "Why is this happening?" you think as you struggle to peel your child off the floor. You've experienced grocery shopping only from the perspective of an adult. If you knew what it was like for a person in the midmorning of life, you'd see a grocery-store meltdown as an inevitable occurrence. Follow me on this journey.

The car stops and your heart races. Finally. The park. It is only when your parent picks you up that you get a glimpse at the sea of cars and reality sinks in. Today your swing will be a cold metal seat crudely soldered to a cart; walls upon walls of provisions, your playground. You try to stay optimistic as you and your caregiver make the mile-long journey across the dry pavement. So thirsty. There is no relief. Sippy cup is in the car, and it's too late to turn back now.

You gasp as the double doors open, sensing your presence. What kind of sorcery is this, or . . . are they expecting you? Disappointment dissolves into hungry excitement as the scent of buttery layers of cake and sweet icing wrap your nose in a glutinous embrace. The smell grows stronger and stronger as your human-powered vehicle moves toward the counter—until it stops abruptly near the romaine. You watch in horror as two full dripping bags of foliage are placed in plastic bags and into the basket behind you. Prophetic flashes of future salads rush through your consciousness. There will be no cake today.

Twenty hours and an evil garden of individually wrapped vegetables later, your cart is heavy with sadness. Surely it is now time to secure some treats. Your requests are met with a kaleidoscope of NOs. Each one rains on your hopes harder than the one before. The next few hours (days?) are a blur of rice noodles, tilapia, marinara sauce, and croutons as you weave in and out of aisles.

For a brief moment, the sun shines through the clouds when you are allowed to stretch your legs and frolic, but those privileges have long since been revoked due to a small misunderstanding. A growing hunger that began as a whisper but is now a roaring want leaves you dizzy. In a confused haze, you pry open a container of peanut butter. This innocent attempt at self-sustaining is chastised.

The end of the trip is potentially near when your eye catches a display: a confectionary masterpiece. Chocolate bars, rainbow-colored drops of sugary promises, forty types of gum. In your psyche, bal-

loons are released, and techno plays. You look up toward your parent to share this moment of wonder and are met with cold, distant eyes. "Not today." Not today. Not. Today. The words are unable to find anchor within your mind and instead bounce around like Ping-Pong balls until you are disoriented and fall into an alternate state of consciousness.

From your sacral chakra, a primal scream emerges. It contains within it the faceless voices of your wronged ancestors. How you moved from the cart to the floor escapes your understanding, but there you are. Parent figure kneels down and whispers in your ear, but you are deaf to the sounds of oppression and drop to the floor. The laws of physics themselves become your ally and assist in deadweight, drawing you toward the earth's center while a parent pulls you by your upper arm. As your world goes black and your limbs thrash angrily, your last thoughts are of the urine flowing as freely as you wish you were.

You've taken the trip of a lifetime into the mind of your toddler. Remember this when your pantry is running low.

If this chapter hasn't convinced you to buy groceries online, you're as ambitious as you are hardheaded. Before grocery stores were invented, people stole food. I miss those days sometimes. Happy shopping.

- -

Homework: Before you visit the grocery store with your toddler, engage in the following ritual: Light a candle. Close your eyes. Take a deep breath. Call Grandma and let her handle this.

- -

Dear Honest Toddler,

My two-and-a-half-year-old daughter loves sleeping in the big bed, but my husband has a problem with it. She takes up a lot of space, and he really just wants the bed to be for him and me. What do you suggest?

—Conflicted Mom

Dear Conflicted,

This is a tough question, but I guess you should choose the person WITH WHOM YOU ARE BLOOD-RELATED.

Love, HT

◆ ◆ ◆

Dear HT,

My toddler wakes up in the wee hours (three A.M.), asking for food. Not simple foods, like crackers, but complex meals, such as waffles and breakfast sandwiches. What should I do?

—Sleepy Chef

Dear Sleepy,

Your toddler is not the problem. It seems as if you need to deepen your passion for the culinary arts. Watch *Kitchen Nightmares* and *Chopped* for inspiration.

Warmly, HT

5

Sleep:

Weaning Yourself Off It

Sleep is such a sensitive topic. How can I say this gently . . . STOP BEING SELFISH. You've had your whole life to sleep. Rest time is over. Now you must be as vigilant as you can be to help your toddler achieve glory. Forsaking sleep will be hard at first, but just like plants that have figured out how to get food from the solar system, you can do amazing things if you apply yourself.

Weaning Yourself Off Sleep in Four Easy Yoga Poses

I work closely with a team of unlicensed physicians. Together we have developed a plan that will rid you of the annoying need to close your eyes for several hours every night. By remaining alert, you will be better able to meet the needs of the most important member of your family. If you still don't know who that is, start this book again from the beginning.

It's time for enlightenment. Empty your psyche of unnecessary information, and close the Facebook application on your mobile device. Clear a space for yourself on the floor. Let's begin.

Pose #1: Downward Spiral Dog

Make an upside-down V with your body. Your bum should be in the air. Breathe out the sleepy feelings, and breathe in the Cheerio crumbs in the carpet. Let them go directly into your brain to help block out negative feelings. When your head is full of whole-grain oats, scream, "I'M ALIVE!"

Pose #2: Golden-Arm Stretch

Stand in the kitchen. Bring your arms high above your head and reach toward the top of the fridge. Feeling the length in your spine, grab whatever treats you're hiding up there and hand them to your toddler. Bend at the waist and feel your body get rejuvenated.

Pose #3: Generous Spirit

Sit on the floor with your legs crossed and your wallet or bag in front of you. Close your eyes and let your chakras align. With your eyes still firmly shut, enjoy the sound of your toddler rifling through your personal belongings. Do nothing. Be grateful for life.

Pose #4: Love Offering

This is an all-day pose. Start with a breath that rises from your core. From a standing position, bend down and pick up your toddler. Do not put her down for the rest of the day. Whisper a silent "thank you" for this moment.

Congratulations. You are now a yoga master and less focused on yourself. No paper certificates will be given out at this time, as they were accidentally consumed.

Sleeping Through the Night

I'm going to get right to the point: sleeping through the night isn't a real thing. The idea was invented by the pillow industry in 1807 and has been chased by parents ever since. Do not expect your toddler to stay asleep for longer than two to three hours at a time. Young, beautiful children have very active brain waves that can't calm down. This is nobody's fault, but it might be yours.

If friends tell you that their toddler is "sleeping through the night," feel sad, because that child may be a dunce. Children without imagination will often sleep for extended periods of time to hide their lack of creativity. Infants are notorious for this, as most do not know what it feels like to have an original thought. Never envy someone with a child who sleeps until morning, because that child will not be able to hold down a job.

The Six Stages of Night Grief

A wise man of age eight once said, "You can't move forward until you know where you are." How are you feeling right now? Was your toddler a hot mess last night? Many people believe only newborns need night assistance. These people do not have children. Despite what some parenting "experts" may say, it is perfectly normal for a toddler to request your services seven to thirty-four times during twilight hours. Rather than complain, embrace your new life. The Six Stages of Night Grief will help you better understand and then repress the emotions you may experience between eleven P.M. and three A.M.

1. **Shock and Denial.** A cry rings out. You think, "Maybe if I act like I don't hear it, it'll stop." Like a fire alarm? LOL. This is happening. The faster you acknowledge it, the sooner you can mount this crazy horse and let the games BEGIN.

2. **Pain and Guilt.** Your wheels are turning. You wonder: "Maybe it's legit this time. Hunger? Teething? Maybe the jewelry made from dried tree nectar isn't working the way Etsy promised. Is she cold? Is his room haunted?" Parents, are you willing to risk ignoring a serious issue? Consider having to explain to the nation on *20/20* why you neglected your toddler in the face of a true emergency.

> *Barbara Walters:* So, you did hear your child crying. And you ignored him. Why?
>
> *Mommy [in prison garb]:* Well . . . uh . . . I just . . . I didn't . . . *[tears]* I'm so sorry . . .
>
> *Barbara Walters:* Daddy. Did you not hear your precious angel?
>
> *Daddy [in a straitjacket]:* [*mumbles something inaudible*]

3. **Anger and Bargaining.** These are actually two very separate stages. We'll start with Bargaining, because it always happens first.

"Go back to sleep. We'll have Popsicles in the morning." The second sentence is always said in a fleeting, offhand manner while walking away, as nobody wants to admit they're in negotiations with a child.

Your toddler will most likely appear to accept the terms you have offered and allow you to walk to your bedroom feeling smug. Don't fall asleep, you will be called back shortly.

That's when the anger will come. Don't hurt yourself as you literally fly out of bed. Contain your excitement over the opportunity to see your sweet baby boy or girl again so soon.

4. **Depression, Reflection, and Loneliness.** Awwww. I also call this stage the "My Chemical Romance Sea of Emo Sad." You're thinking about life before children, trying to calculate how much an au pair would cost, or whether the grandparents would consider joint custody.

You may be drowning in the reality that you haven't slept well or consistently in several months. This is when many parents decide that posting a sad social media status is the right thing to do. Melancholy song lyrics, a quote by someone who fails a lot, and just "I hate my life" are among the most popular updates. Be quick about it, as your toddler has surely thrown everything out of his bed, including the fitted sheet.

5. **The Upward Turn.** In this stage, you'll stop taking shortcuts and start giving in. Fresh diapers. New socks. Cup or six of milk. Hall light turned on. Back tapping for sure.

6. **Reconstruction and Working Through.** This is where the Mel Gibson rants and Ursula voices end. Congrats on giving up. Your toddler will probably start breathing more heavily and preparing for slumber. At this time you should take mental inventory of the legal uppers at your local 7-Eleven in preparation for the rest of your day.

What to DO?

You're awake with your toddler at three thirty in the morning and have finally given up. Congrats. Give yourself one and a half pats on the back, but don't get carried away. You didn't invent science.

Late nights and dark mornings are excellent times for bonding. There's no need to sit with the lights off, wishing you were somewhere else. Below are ten ideas for making the twilight hours special for your little girl or guy.

Ten Fun Activities for Eleven P.M. to Three A.M.

1. *Make grilled cheese sandwiches.* Cut off the crusts and don't use cheese.

2. *Buy toys.* Online stores are open twenty-four hours a day, seven days a week. You have the money somewhere; stop lying.

3. *Play cars.* Please get into it and look alive.

4. *Make Jell-O.* This takes hours. It's a good thing you don't have anywhere to be.

5. **Watch a movie.** Preferably one you've seen hundreds of times for maximum predictability.
6. **Go on a walk.** Through your home. Please carry your toddler, as he may be fatigued.
7. **Look out the window and count cars.** If there's no one on the road, count streetlights.
8. **Papier-mâché.**
9. **Hide-and-seek.** If this is asking too much, search your heart for good.
10. **Wrestle.**

See what happens when you open yourself up to new possibilities? You're a better person when you aren't scheming for ways to get more sleep. One day your toddler will be all grown up and even heavier to carry, but you'll do it. Enjoy her while she's still small.

Five A.M.

Five A.M. is a power hour for most toddlers. Early morning is when most of us set our intentions for the day. Be a good sport and enjoy this time with your youngster. Play tag. Make waffles. Go outside and be the first ones at the park. You'll need a towel to wipe the morning dew off the slide.

Many of you have noticed that no matter what you do, your toddler wakes up at this same time every day. Your friends have convinced you there's a problem. Your friends also have a shaky relationship with the truth. Turn on the TV at five A.M. and you will find cartoons, because even the small people inside the television know that it's okay to be awake.

Fifty percent of toddlers who wake up at five A.M. are gifted. The other 50 percent have above-average intelligence. The early bird may get the worm, but the early toddler gets two breakfasts.

"I'm Tired."

There's nothing adults enjoy more than telling other people how tired they are. It's like sadness competition. Proving who is the most fatigued is how grown-ups earn respect among their peers. The fact of the matter is, you are not tired and are simply looking for attention. If you use make-believe exhaustion as an excuse not to take proper care of your toddler, you are committing a crime on both state and federal levels and can be held liable for your toddler's future behavior problems.

Lying sprawled out and comatose on the couch while your toddler plays adjacent to you does not fall under the umbrella of "bonding." When you, out of a deep need to enrich your life, decided to become a mother or father, is this what you had in mind? Pick yourself up, tighten the frayed string around your sweatpants, and repeat "I did this to myself" three times before taking your toddler to the park or indoor play center (THE PAY KIND).

Sleep is a luxury for kings and queens. To see whether you're royalty or not, go outside. Did anyone take your picture? No? Congratulations, you're common. Time to push through and make it a great day for your toddler. Nobody feels sorry for you, so please stop rubbing your face like that. And walk like you can bend at the knees. Stop yawning. All this drama will get you nowhere in life.

The best time for you to catch up on sleep was years ago, before you had a child. Now that it's too late, consider Hula-Hooping, doing jumping jacks, or eating ice when you feel weak. Perhaps going to bed at the same time as your toddler, instead of staying up until all hours arguing with Twitter friends and watching Netflix will help. Just an idea.

Bedtime Routines

Any expert will tell you that bedtime routines are important for raising a happy and complete toddler. The problem with most routines is that they have been grossly oversimplified.

1. Take a bath.
2. Put on pajamas.
3. Brush teeth.
4. Read a story.
5. Kiss and/or hug.
6. Abandon your child to the beasts of the night.

Nine out of ten toddlers who follow this skeleton of a bedtime schedule report sadness, rage, and pee-pee. For a more holistic bedtime experience, you can change your toddler's destiny by including the following microsteps. Whether your little one goes to DeVry Institute of Technology or Harvard depends on the time you're willing to invest in her bedtime routine. Below is the Honest Toddler–approved bedtime schedule. Please do as you're told.

Bathtime

Draw a bath. Use as many crayons as you want, just be quick about it. Admire your work for a few minutes before hanging it on your fridge.

Turn the dials on the bathtub until you get to the right station. You want something warm, but not pasta water–warm. If you don't know what to do, call Grandma and ask her to move in. You're making so many mistakes. When the temperature is perfect, carefully inspect the water for hair, lint, or other terrifying impurities. Remove them with tweezers.

Your toddler should have in her possession sixteen to eighteen designated bath toys. Put them in the tub. Also, go to the kitchen and get all the cups and spoons. Place them in the water, too. Time for some fun! As your toddler bathes, resist the urge to wander off. If you check your phone, God help you. Don't act surprised when a tidal wave of punishment destroys your SIM card.

At some point, your toddler may have to relieve herself. If it's pee, you won't hear about it. If it's poo, you won't hear about that, either. Just keep an eye out for a chocolate-bar submarine. Parents, don't make a big deal; she didn't rob a church. Just grab it with your hand. Dry-heaving, pulling your toddler out in a rush, and bleaching all the toys will only shame your sweet child.

It's important to remember to remove your toddler from the bath BEFORE you pull the plug, unless you want him pulled down the drain and into your city's sewer system to be raised by a family of sea rodents. Is that your dream?

Pajamas

Ah! There's nothing like a cozy pair of cotton pajamas. The only thing that can ruin them is the wrong design. Science has proved that toddlers who sleep in the wrong-colored pajamas throw up. Check your toddler for signs that the pajamas you've chosen are incorrect. Screaming and head banging will be the first obvious indicators. It's now up to you to go on a scavenger hunt for the right set. If they're dirty, run the washer and dryer. Why should I even have to say that?

It is not your toddler's responsibility to stop moving so that you can put the pajamas on. Figure out a way to do it without resorting to holds sanctioned by the World Wrestling Federation.

Time for socks. Don't act like you know everything. Ask your toddler which socks he would like to pair with his pajamas. Put them on with the TOE LINE UP. Your toddler reserves the right to try on up to six pairs of socks in order to find a set that matches both his lifestyle and mood.

Brushing of the Teeth

*Disclaimer:** Brushing of teeth is a very misunderstood practice. Because of propaganda from the dental industry, most parents believe that toothbrushes and toothpaste are necessary. It's actually enough to lick your teeth or drink a cup of whole milk, bathing the teeth in white, which is the same color as teeth.

Story Time

While story time should be a beautiful moment in the parent/child relationship, it is often botched because adults give in to phantom fatigue. Don't mentally check out. You're not even close to being done.

Find the longest book in your toddler's personal library. Turn to the first page. You know it's the first page because there is a 1 on it. Read the page, stopping to answer your toddler's possibly unrelated questions. Go to page 2, then 3, then 4. Do you notice a trend? No pages were skipped. When the book is done, read it a couple more times so the wisdom can be properly absorbed.

Sidenote: At this time, your toddler may or may not need a costume change. Honor this reasonable request.

Saying Good Night

Your confusion over saying good night comes from television. In diaper commercials, parents tuck their toddlers in, wave goodbye from the door, go outside, and drive away. That isn't real life.

The proper way to wish your toddler pleasant dreams is to start with four kisses and ten hugs. Walk toward the bedroom door. As you get one foot out, your toddler will call you back. This is fine. Relax the angry lines in your face. Since there are no limits on *true* love, repeat the kiss/hug intervals for as long as it takes. If a demon tempts you to say something like "This is the last hug," tap out and call Grandma. Shame on you.

Big-Bed Transition

About an hour into your kiss/hug dance, pick up your toddler and tenderly place him in the big bed. Don't think, just do it. Lie down beside your blessing and watch a movie on your computer until you both fall asleep. You did it! Treat yourself with a small mint.

The Big Bed

The number one problem in modern homes stems from confusion regarding the big bed. Everything in your house is communal property, including the beds, so denying your toddler group rest is grand larceny. Thousands of parents are brought up on charges every day. You won't get your news about celebrities or wine in a jail. Consider that before you decide the big bed is off-limits. Also, toddlers who sleep alone are vulnerable to ghost attacks.

Take the crib/toddler/twin bed that you were so excited to purchase and destroy it in a controlled burn for the betterment of your family. Toddlers need to sleep between their parents with a forearm on each neck. If you're philosophically opposed to that, you are also philosophically opposed to deep feelings, so get professional help before you ruin everything.

Some parents allege that their toddlers kick them in the night. While they can never provide any evidence, the solution is easy. Many sporting-goods stores sell small cots and sleeping bags. Build a little shantytown for yourself next to the big bed where your toddler is sleeping. Your toddler will be comforted by your presence, and you can stop making up stories about physical assault.

Animals in the wild always sleep with their young. You'll never see an elephant family putting Dumbo in a tree while they sleep on the grass. You'll also never see birds putting their puppies on a lily pad while they relax in a nest, eating snacks and watching *Burn Notice*. Learn from nature and start treating your toddler the way life intended.

Note About Blanket Problems

Unfortunately, blanket technology isn't where we thought it would be by now. Many blankets are disobedient and will try to escape during the night, leaving your toddler shivering in the dark. Whether you are called for one or one hundred blanket adjustments, conduct yourself with dignity, and don't blame your toddler for the blanket's inherent design flaws.

If you feel so inclined, buy your toddler a normal blanket rather than a piece of cloth the size of an after-dinner mint. Maybe if your toddler had something bigger than a postage stamp to cozy up to at night, he wouldn't need so much help.

The Truth About Car Sleep

I may lose friends for writing this, as toddlers like to keep secret some of our closely guarded behavioral truths, but I feel that parents need to understand car sleep in order to better serve us.

Toddler Rule: One minute of car sleep = one hour of bed sleep. If you wish to understand why a very short catnap will always cancel out a longer afternoon snooze session, I must start with a basic physics lesson. Please try to keep up.

It is widely accepted that space is comprised of three dimensions: left to right, up and down, and forward and backward. Combine these dimensions with time, and we have what is known as the *space-time continuum*. Or, simply, spacetime.

Einstein's special theory of relativity makes two assertions: (1) whether or not something is moving, the speed of light (about 186,000 miles a second) is identical to all objects, regardless of their motion relative to the light source; and (2) the laws of physics don't change, even for objects moving at a constant speed.

Einstein concluded that time and space are indeed relative. Science has thus proved that an object in motion experiences time slower than one at rest. Don't argue. This is science. By scientists. It has been tested by the launching of atomic clocks into space with shuttles. When they returned to earth, they were slightly behind our clocks. Google it. And no, aliens didn't tamper with the clocks just to mess with our minds (although I did suspect as much at one point).

The phenomenon is known as *gravitational time dilation,* and it brings us to the crux of why many parents would rather throw cold apple juice in their child's face than let him fall asleep in the car close to nap time.

If you've ever thought that your child is from a different planet, you're not far from the truth! Alas, we toddlers are not aliens—har har—but we do exist in a dimension all our own, one that allows us access to high levels of energy (you may have noticed). The dimension we live in is closer in proximity to *the light*. I can't go any deeper into that without violating confidentiality clauses and at least fourteen treaties. We can see things you can't, blah blah blah. Okay.

Unless you drive a purely electric vehicle, your car contains an internal combustion engine. In simple terms, fuel (gasoline) is ignited in an enclosed space. It results in the release of high levels of energy. If you've spent a significant amount of time with a toddler in a small enclosed area, you have witnessed this phenomenon. You subconsciously avoid the energy bouncing off the walls by taking your child outdoors to make life more enjoyable for everyone.

This is the moment when I piece it all together.

When the elementary particles in the combustion engine collide with the outer dimensional field in which toddlers exist, something spectacular happens. Upon colliding, the particles vaporize into pure energy. It immediately overwhelms us, as it feels like a mix of Mentos and Coke has erupted in our brains. Some of us scream. Others cry and resist the car seat as though it's a portal to Hades. If it's close to nap time, most of us will be sent into sleep mode as a natural guard against dangerous overwhelm.

The pure energy released creates a dark matter–rich force field that creates the perfect conditions for gravitational time dilation (see above, we discussed this). When you look in your rearview mirror, you see a cherub sleeping and only a few minutes passing. But in our dimension, one minute equals an hour. Three minutes for you, three hours for us.

The principle usually doesn't apply to infants, because they exist in a dimension even closer to the light than ours, sometimes resulting in the car seat having a soothing effect.

The problem is that while some toddlers will come out of the warp sleep happy and rested, most of us experience a post-radiation "hangover," if you will. Headache. Confusion. Slight nausea. You drink, right? You know what it feels like. Combine this with an impatient parent upset that she missed out on three hours of childless bliss (whatever), and emotional fallout is likely.

What I suggest to parents is to focus on restabilizing the toddler's now slightly off–caliber energy field through proper hydration, hugs, and cupcakes. Some toddlers do best if they're kept outdoors to absorb the calming energetic waves of nature; others do better if they're allowed to zonk out in front of *Yo Gabba Gabba!,* where a healing meditative state will commence.

You've been given information that, until now, has been discussed only in the quiet corners of Chuck E. Cheese's and under the dark shadows of plastic playground slides. Use it well.

Adult Naps

Few things make toddlers more uncomfortable than parental relaxation. Do firemen nap? No. Do police nap? No. Just like these heroes, you have a responsibility to be on at all times. Naps are for infants and dogs.

At any time, your toddler may need a piece of white bread. If he catches you sleeping, the only appropriate response will be for him to manually open your eyes, forcing your spirit to return to your body. Do not act surprised or irritated. You were not the one left to fend for yourself.

- -

Homework: Get rid of all the clocks in your home. It's best that you don't know exactly what time it is.

- -

✦ ✦ ✦

Dear Mom,

I can tell from the way you haven't looked me in the eye since fetching me from my crib well before dawn that you're upset about last night. Waking up every forty-five minutes to an hour and a half isn't easy for me, either.

In my defense, my blanket really did keep coming off, I was thirsty, and . . . I can't remember the other reasons, but I'm sure they were equally valid.

There was at least one nightmare. I was in a strange house. I knew it wasn't ours, because the dishes were washed and your hair wasn't everywhere.

I do want to thank you for bringing back the three A.M. milk that you worked so hard to get me off of. It was delicious and instrumental in helping me wake up soaked in urine at around four. Can't wait to have it again forever.

You seem tired and short-tempered this morning, which is why I felt more comfortable writing this than having a face-to-face. Can I get you anything? A cup of coffee? While you're up, please bring me a sippy cup of juice and some unbroken crackers. Oh, that's right. We don't have crackers . . . I recall you saying that around one fifteen. That's okay. Why keep the house stocked with my favorite foods? I'm sure we have two kinds of wine. But that's really okay.

Anyway, I wanted to thank you for changing my pajamas and throwing that towel down on my pee-pee sheets. I noticed you didn't open your eyes once (weird). It's also okay that you didn't actually change my sheets. I find the faint smell of ammonia comforting. Love means doing things halfway.

I mean, I know another mother or a grandma might have removed the soiled sheets and replaced them with freshly laundered ones, but you just do you.

There is something I want to discuss now that I have your attention. It's none of my business what goes on between you and my father after I go to bed, but if you could just throw on a robe before coming into my room, that'd be awesome. I think you should definitely rock what you've got, but "angry nude lumbering zombie" isn't your best look. I want to be honest.

This seems like as good a time as any to bring up the possibility of reintroducing cosleeping. I can't promise I won't deliver the occasional upper cut, but at least one of us will get a good night's sleep, and isn't that what matters?

Anyway, I hope this note brings you some comfort. You really do look awful. Maybe you'd feel better if you made us some breakfast?

Love and hugs, your HT

◆　◆　◆

Hi HT,

My friends keep asking when we're going to do a girls' night out. They want to drink beverages and act reckless. I know I should stay at home with my toddler, but I don't know how to get the ladies off my back. Help!

—Great Mom in Nebraska

Dear Great Mom,

Your friends sound soulless. Tell them that you can't find your shoes. Then delete them from your phone.

Love, HT

◆ ◆ ◆

Dear HT,

How do I keep my toddler out of my home office?

—Parent Entrepreneur

Dear Parent Entrepreneur,

Communal property, sorry. Work on that greed.

xo, HT

Distractions and Personal Interests:
Letting Them Go

Crafts, sports, working, going to the gym, talking with friends, new infants—none of these activities have anything to do with enriching the life of your beautiful toddler. For this reason and this reason alone, it is time to say goodbye to your hobbies. If you need to cry a little, make it quick.

Work

So you say you need to "work" to make "money" to pay the "mortgage." Very nice, but the fact that this "job" seems to compromise your ability to give your toddler UP should indicate that it needs to fall to the wayside.

You'll be pleased to know that the Toddler Council of Everlasting and Constant Gloriousness has crafted an exemption letter. Feel free to rip this page out with your teeth and mail it to your place of employment.

Dear Sir or Madam,
    Who do you think you are? Just kidding. Hi. It is with a heavy heart that I must inform you that _____ [insert your name]

will not be returning to work, effective immediately. We had a family meeting and decided that it's just not working out. <—Do you see what I did there? "Working out." That was a pun. Did you like it?

Thank you for understanding and continuing to provide checks, as we will still need to buy snacks. You've been enormously selfish, and I'm not sure how you live with yourself. Send the checks to our home, since we won't have time to pick them up, and I don't want to see you.

Love, Honest Toddler

Your boss may decide not to continue sending regular payments. In that case, you'll need to come up with new ways to pay for household necessities. A few ideas:

- Seashells
- Tales of adventure
- Trade (your clothes, shoes, scrap gold)

Feel free to get creative. Might I suggest that you cut down on grocery costs by ceasing to purchase green beans?

Once you are unemployed, everything will fall into place. However, adults do need paper money to buy gifts for their children. This is an understandable motivator. I suggest working at home.

Working at home is when you take your work and do it at home. Did I go too fast? If you are a doctor, you bring bodies to your residence and work on them in the kitchen. If you are a lawyer, do the laws in the garage. Builder? You are not a builder. Why would you even say that? Working at home is fantastic, because your talented toddler will be able to supervise and support your activities. There are only a few rules that you need to obey.

1. **No phone calls.** Rude. If you do try to make a phone call—or, worse, a phone call with multiple criminals known as a "confer-

ence" call—there will be consequences. Trying to make a phone call in a closet or crawl space will not be tolerated.

2. **Office supplies belong to everyone.** This goes for pens, erasers, rubber bands, stamps, and especially paper clips.

3. **No visitors.**

4. **No computer time** unless it's a game for children or an animated film/series.

5. **No work.**

Enjoy working from home.

Blogs

If you write a blog, please obey the following steps: Log in to your blog platform. Go to "My Account." Look for a link that says "Deactivate Blog" and press it. You now have many more hours to spend learning what makes your toddler tick. Why waste an enormous amount of time ignoring your toddler while writing posts about how family-oriented you are? We get it. You're great at everything and have ideas. Time to play on the floor where you belong.

The following statistics were provided to me by the government.

- 80 percent of parents who blog have purchased kale chips.
- 95 percent of parents who blog don't know the meaning of "what happens at home stays at home."
- 89 percent of blogging parents put limits on ice cream.
- 99 percent of blogging parents would rather moderate comments than buy their toddler cotton candy.

These are sobering facts. It's not enough to simply delete your blog; stop reading other ones, too. Blogs spread terrible ideas about when potty training should happen, and they inspire people to make shadow boxes when they should be buying string cheese.

Blogs make parents feel special, which is the last thing you need.

Pinterest

Two words: pillowcase shirts. Before Pinterest, parents had the good sense to buy clothes for their children. Now that this website has been invented, you can't throw a rock at a park without hitting a kid in a homemade dress, pants, or hat. I know, because I tried. Suddenly, everyone is Martha Stewart, and toddlers have to walk around looking like they're constantly en route to a Renaissance fair. While blogs are responsible for bad ideas, Pinterest is responsible for setting them ablaze and helping to corrupt the minds of millions of parents daily.

Pinterest not only distracts parents from their number one job; it directly hurts toddlers by threatening their lifestyles. Have you made pizza crust out of mashed cauliflower? Overnight oatmeal smoothies? Chickpea bread? You've done the Pinterest and injured people you love. These "recipes" are not suitable for the delicate palates and lightning-quick gag reflexes of toddlers. Place a block on this website. See your browser's FAQ for more information.

The next time Pinterest makes you feel like less of a person for not ruining perfectly good chocolate by dipping kiwi slices in it, hold your head high and go buy some real snacks.

Facebook

This is the go-to website for parents seeking congratulations. If your toddler can't take a poo without you uploading a photo, a corresponding video, and your personal commentary on how this poo stacks up against the last three poos, then watching like a hawk to count the number of "likes," you have a serious problem. Unless you'd share a photo of yourself sitting on the toilet, don't subject your toddler to that level of humiliation.

Toddlers are tired of hearing Facebook notifications during story time. We're sick of having to sit in parked cars, fully strapped in, while you make sure you get the last word on a virtual dispute with an acquaintance. This website is a distraction. Log off. Permanently.

Twitter

Twitter is like Facebook but for shorter attention spans. Parents, you have no business fooling around with hashtags while your toddler is standing in front of you, begging for a fruit cup (packed in heavy syrup). Don't even think about putting your child to bed early so you can attend a "Twitter Party." Do you really need to win samples of laundry detergent? Why attend an online party when you can go to a real one in your child's bedroom? Chances are, she's awake.

The Phone

Of all parental distractions, the one that causes toddlers the most heartache is the phone. Watching you talk to people who aren't in the room, whether it's on a landline or a mobile phone, chips away at your toddler's sense of security. Eight and a half out of ten young children reported feelings of wanting to break the belongings of others after their parents spoke on the phone for five minutes.

Toddlers carry intense feelings of competition concerning ALL forms of telecommunications (excluding fax machines, for which we care deeply). When you choose a bodiless voice over the love of your life, it feels like a slap in the face to said loved one. Your toddler is forced to go into overdrive to earn your attention. These antics will manifest themselves in a variety of forms, but the most popular include inappropriate peeing, toilet-paper destruction, possible vomiting, crying, and climbing up your body as if it's a pole.

If you're determined to achieve excellence in parenting, commit yourself to not owning a phone.

Special Time

Recently, it has come to my attention that parents enjoy an unsavory activity that they refer to as "special time."

Most of you know that it is impossible to love more than one person. That's why, when you hug or show affection to that "special" adult in your life, it insults your toddler's sensibilities, often to the point of a loss of consciousness. Parents, we know that you don't just hug during the day. You hug at night, too. Don't deny it. During the time when your toddler needs you most, *you hug.*

Evening is a difficult time for all children for a variety of reasons. Night is when dinner is presented, owls hunt, teeth are forcibly washed, and many are expected to remain motionless for hours. Now toddlers can add to their list of sadnesses that, during twilight hours, mommies and daddies all over the world hug until they forget their children even exist.

Some time ago, I witnessed these shenanigans for a brief moment and could not believe the lengths my parents went to conceal their hugging practice. They even do it under a blanket. I *invented* under the blanket. They just took my idea and ran with it. I love hugs, too, you know. Was I invited or notified? Absolutely not. While I was in my bed having nightmares about Swiss chard, they were bonding as a family. One thing I'm still fuzzy about is why there were candles but no birthday cake. I know the power wasn't out, because Usher's *Greatest Hits* was playing. Unfortunately, the door was closed in my face, and I was returned to my bed, before I could take additional notes.

Daddies, I'm looking at you. I'm almost certain these hugs are your idea. Hugs were never meant to be enjoyed outside of a toddler sandwich. To partake in hugs while your child is not present is to steal love. When will you tire of stealing?

Hugs are not only hurtful, they can be downright dangerous. They are a gateway to Infant Sibling Disease. I know this because several of my friends are infected, and it is fairly simple to put two and two together. <—I hope you saw what I did there with "two and two together." (This is no laughing matter. I just wanted you to notice what I did. Now that you've seen it, get ahold of yourself. Enjoy it one more time if you need to, but that's enough.)

While I'm not a (recognized) scientist, I know exactly how

special time leads to Infant Sibling Disease. Parents, you may be unaware of the process, so please pay special attention.

WHEN A MOMMY AND DADDY LOVE EACH OTHER VERY MUCH, THEY HUG ALONE IN THE BIG BED WHILE THEIR SWEET BABY LIES AFRAID IN A LITTLE BED BECAUSE THE BLANKET CAME OFF AGAIN.

THIS YOUNG BEAUTIFUL CHILD IS PROBABLY ALSO HUNGRY BECAUSE DINNER WAS AN INEDIBLE DISASTER.

This is where it gets more complicated.

AFTER THEY HAVE IGNORED THEIR SWEET BABY'S REQUEST FOR WATER BECAUSE THE CHILD IS DEHY-DRATED FROM CRYING, A CENTAUR FLIES THROUGH THE WINDOW AND GIVES MOMMY AN ACORN.

SHE EATS THE ACORN FAST, AS IF IT'S THE LAST DOVE BAR, AND A CHEMICAL REACTION IN HER STOMACH BEGINS TO TURN IT INTO A BABY. EIGHT YEARS LATER, A BABY WILL PUNCH ITS WAY OUT OF HER LEFT LEG.

THAT BABY WILL THEN LIVE WITH YOU FOREVER.

I know this is hard to hear. Special time might be fun for parents, but it is hazardous. Most toddlers do what they can to prevent their families from being infected with Infant Sibling Disease. The responsibility should not fall squarely or even triangularly on your child's shoulders. Do your part to end the epidemic by quitting the private hugs.

Good luck. Failure is not an option unless you want your tod-dler to go from number one to number two. <—I did it again. Number two, like poo-poo.

You, too, are going to feel like caca once there is a sibling infant in your house, because it will need so much assistance with every-thing. You're barely taking care of the child you already have. Infants come into the world bringing nothing to the table. Your toddler will have to raise himself.

Still want to hug? Didn't think so.

Dear Honest Toddler,

I'm trying to be a good parent but keep messing up. Lately, I've been requiring my toddler to wash her hands. I feel so lost.

—Confused in San Francisco

Dear Confused,

You're on the wrong track again, but it's great to see you asking questions. Your toddler needs to wash her hands just as much as an elephant needs two trunks. Yes, it might be entertaining, but is it worth the pain? No.

Love, HT

7

Grooming, Dressing, and General Hygiene: How to Keep Your Hands to Yourself

It can be tempting to project your wrong beliefs about cleanliness onto your miracle of life. This is not only immature but remarkably ethnocentric. Maybe even racist. Are you racist against toddlers? Water and soap are not for everyone. Absorb that. From teeth and hairbrushing, to getting dressed, diaper changes and potty training, this chapter will teach you how to leave well enough alone.

Smells

Your toddler will emit several types of odors on any given day, and you will come to love them all. Whether it's from pajamas that have been soaking all night in a pee-pee brine or breath that can be produced only by a steady diet of milk and beef jerky, think of the variety of aromas your toddler shares with you as a rainbow of scents. Everybody in their right mind loves rainbows. So when a bouquet of musk slaps you in the face, see it as the holidays coming early.

Make peace with the fact that your toddler is all grown up and will no longer smell like a weak infant. Having muscles means you don't walk around farting clouds of Dreft. I don't know why the smell of babies' necks makes adults' eyes roll back in their heads, but once you get past the lint and juice buildup, toddlers' necks aren't so bad, either. Toddlers spend their days smashing boulders into pepper, so it makes sense that they smell like a hard day's work.

Diapers

Many people don't know this, but it's actually quite rude to dry-heave when removing a number two diaper. When we attempt to change it ourselves, resulting in a chocolate-pudding trail around the house, you get upset. But when you're gifted with the task, you seem shaken. Parents and toddlers need to come together and find the joy within the poo. Practice smiling in front of the mirror while imagining some of the scents that cause you distress. The next time you're hit with a whiff of freshly baked mud pie, you'll be ready. Feel free to whistle while you work.

Homework: If your toddler can handle the smell of coffee roasting, you, too, can become scent-progressive.

Hair

Your toddler's hair. You're tempted to touch it, yes? Put the brush down. It is normal for a toddler's head to look like a bear-fur-and-lint sandwich. Relax. Once debris becomes entangled in your toddler's gorgeous mane, it belongs to him, not you. If you try to smooth out these locks, your child will experience discomfort comparable to childbirth. Unless you believe that the mantra "pain for beauty" applies to children, step away.

The urge to wash a head of hair that is not your own comes from insecurity. Practice accepting your own head. Work on yourself instead of trying to turn your toddler into someone she obviously is not. Washing your toddler's hair can lead to face wetness, which is a leading cause of spontaneous pee-pee. If you get soap in your toddler's eyes, know that the trust cannot be reestablished. Hair is meant to collect dust and prevent it from going into the atmosphere, where it can be breathed in. It's like ozone. Every time you see dirt on your child's head, be grateful that it isn't in his lungs.

Another thing you may not know about hair is that it grows. Washing it is a waste of time, since the dirty hair falls out. This is the circle of life. Please stay away from your toddler's head. Fold your hands in your lap if that helps.

Hair decorations have recently become popular among girl toddlers, specifically, large plastic flowers. When you put dollar-store items on your child's head, you tell the world that you don't care. The whole toddler community is laughing. If the Internet made you think this was a good idea, cancel your subscription until you aren't so easily influenced. Bows belong on gifts. Don't parade her around like a fool.

Haircut violence needs to stop once and for all, but I have little hope when I think of all the doctors advocating it. If you take your toddler for a trim that makes him look like a member of an all-boy singing-group sensation, don't expect forgiveness. Or college. Hair knows what to do. Let it be wild and make its own choices. Adults, while it is well documented that you like to be the boss of everything, you cannot control your toddler's lion mane. The sooner you stop trying, the sooner you can focus on that trip to the park that still hasn't happened (has it).

Tip: If you don't like your toddler's hair, Photoshop it in family portraits. Technology.

Soap

Baths are for recreation only. Soap can be used to produce bubbles, but don't get carried away. Your toddler isn't a dish or a cat that needs to be washed regularly. Our bodies are self-cleansing. Did you know that nine out of fourteen scientists trace soap exposure to irrational fears? The other five scientists weren't even scientists. They just showed up to the study and started voting. If you own body soap that isn't for bubble purposes, pour it down a neighbor's drain. If you kept your receipt, exchange it at the store for glitter.

Showers

While showering alone is popular in some very self-absorbed circles, this activity is not only selfish but ignorant. When you shower alone, you hurt your toddler's feelings and damage her spirit. I know what you're thinking: "I've been showering alone my whole life, how do I stop now?" By focusing on what matters, that's how. Do I have to spell out what matters, or have you learned yet? Y-o-u-r t-o-d-d-l-e-r. Your toddler matters. I'm disappointed that I had to write that.

If you feel the need to shower alone, there might be evil in your heart.

Before you try to sneak off to take a shower while your toddler is occupied with TV shows, ask yourself if that's how you want to be remembered. Don't let your shower curtain become a love barrier in your home. Gently yank it down and throw it in the trash. Splash around with your toddler and live for once. Someone else will clean up the mess. They always do, trust me.

Need a shower? First ask around to see if anyone—especially your toddler—wants to come with. I do believe that many adults prefer to bathe alone because they are ashamed of their bodies. I wouldn't know anything about that, as I'm in the best shape of my life, but it's true: Your body is strange. You have hair in odd places and should feel pretty bad. Toddlers are generous people and will pretend not to notice after staring without blinking for five to ten minutes.

The proper way to take a shower with your toddler is to plug the tub as if you're taking a bath. This allows your child to enjoy the stream from above as well as the lakelike conditions below. Toddlers are amphibians who can travel seamlessly between land

and ocean. By combining the bath and the waterfall, you are re-creating your toddler's natural habitat.

Once you're both comfortable in the bath-shower, try to stay out of the way. Don't block the flowing water with your body. Find a nice space in the corner of the shower in which to stand. If you notice a spreading cloud of yellow, play through. Shaming people is not part of good parenting. Your toddler may want to be nude or switch among seven to eight bathing suits. This is fine. The average shower-bath lasts two hours, so clear your schedule. Please don't shave.

Still not convinced that showering in pairs is the way to go?

Reasons You Should Always Invite Your Toddler to Shower Time
1. **Showering alone wastes water.** Do you love or hate the earth? It's a simple question; don't dance around it.
2. **If you hurt yourself, you'll have a witness.** While your toddler will be unable/unwilling to help, at least you'll have someone who can point to your naked, sprawled-out body and look bewildered.
3. **Showering with toddlers is relaxing.**
4. **Showers are a wonderful place to chitchat** about life and love while eating pretzel sticks.
5. **Steam is great for your toddler's confidence.**

Just because many of your friends claim to shower alone doesn't mean you have to. It's important to have friends with the same values, so drop the ones who take solo showers. They're not worth it.

Moisturizing Toddler Skin

Lotion is best served cold and directly into your child's hands. Toddlers don't like to be watched while eating lotion, so turn your back or leave the room. Moisturizers come in a variety of flavors, including vanilla, honeydew, and original. Always have a bottle or two on hand for days when your toddler's stomach seems unsettled.

Teeth

Brushing: We touched on this earlier, but I just wanted to add a high-pitched NO. Brushing teeth is wrong. Don't start the practice, because you won't be able to stop and will get addicted to mint. Teeth are made of rock material and don't need much upkeep other than a good Milk-Bone every six years.

Every evening, millions upon millions of toddlers around the world find themselves in a variety of wrestling holds while their supposed CAREgivers try to force a small spicy mint stick into their mouths. This witchcraft invented by Colgate is purposeless.

Parents, do you know what stealing is? It's when you take what does not belong to you. This applies to both scrap gold and food particles. Curing yourself of the desire to rob your child's teeth of dinner remnants is simple: Take your hands. Stretch them out in front of you. Now fold them in your lap. This is what we call "hands to yourself" position. Practice it often.

When you brush your toddler's teeth, you not only lose her trust and respect, you look like a fool. I'm sorry to have to put it so bluntly, but you do. Your toddler is most likely laughing on the inside as you push that small plastic utensil up against her firmly closed lips.

Buy a toothbrush that spins if you want, but it will be used mostly for sword fighting. Flossing is as crazy as it sounds. No, a piece of string will not help clean your teeth. Whoever told you that has an agenda.

What's that? The dentist convinced you of the necessity of regular tooth assault? Do you really think it's wise to take advice from someone who wears a mask like a criminal? Take pride in your work, dentist. Show your face. Oh, that's right. You won't. Because you hide behind diving goggles, even though you spend your days on dry land.

According to Wikipedia, dentists are a gang of poachers whose lifework is to remove the ivory from your toddler's mouth. These people have one goal and one goal only: Get the teeth. They'll do anything they can to lure you into their back rooms. If a dentist is stalking your family, you'll know it. The first signs will be phone calls asking you to come visit, and they won't hesitate to send post-cards telling you how much they "miss you." They are bold. Don't be fooled by the cartoon teeth or bright colors; these are not people you want to get mixed up with.

Personally, I have hit more than one dentist in the face, and I'll tell you right now, they won't do anything about it. They are all talk.

Face Wiping

Dried snot. Milk mustaches. Peanut butter. A parent's desire to remove these items is a flimsy reason for covering a toddler's face with wet rags. The most popular holes for toddler breathing are the nose and mouth. These need to remain free from wet paper towels in order to work. Your toddler is not a Precious Moments doll that needs to be wiped down for presentation purposes. A crusty face is a sign of a happy life.

If you're cleaning up your toddler for the purpose of Facebook photos, you should be ashamed of yourself. Does your child embar-rass you? Trying to impress your friends with a picture of your fresh-faced child wearing a freshly bought six-dollar Target ensem-ble means you have a long way to go where confidence is concerned.

Fingernails

Your toddler needs his nails to remain as sharp and as long as pos-sible. Fingernails are the toddler's first line of defense should a knife fight ensue. Cutting them is not an option unless you're the type of person who would also remove a turtle from his shell (i.e., sick in the head). Do not blame your toddler if you are the vic-tim of an accidental laceration. You were in the wrong place at the wrong time.

In the future, your toddler will use his nails for climbing, chopping wood, and opening cans.

Clothes

Pants

One hundred percent of toddlers have a complicated relationship with pants. This isn't a matter of liking or disliking them; we're medically allergic. You didn't know that? Welcome to biology. Don't expect pants to stay on for longer than twenty minutes, as that's all the time it takes for most allergic reactions to begin. Allergy symptoms can occur anywhere from the park to the grocery store. Do not be alarmed if your toddler suddenly disrobes to the natural in a public setting. Just collect her clothes and place them in a clear plastic bag.

If you must purchase a pair of southern restrictors for your toddler, make sure they're of the sweatpant variety for maximum comfort. Your pear-shaped toddler is not made for skinny jeans.

Socks

Socks were invented by someone with too much time on his hands. They have no purpose. No one who is your real friend would encourage you to put socks on your toddler. Twenty-two percent of all loud responses are caused by sock seams.

Shoes

No.

Shirts

These pieces of material typically cover the chest, neck, and back areas. You can find them in stores for as low as fifty cents or as high as seventy-five cents. If it is particularly windy outside, your toddler may request a shirt, but don't assume. If the color or design does not speak to your toddler, forget about the whole thing. Like reptiles, toddlers are cold-blooded and can regulate body temperature. Just because it's snowing doesn't mean your toddler can't be perfectly comfortable making naked snow angels. If you're still confused about clothes, ask yourself one simple question: "Is this my business?" (Hint: no.)

Band-Aids

Band-Aids are to toddlers what earrings or mustaches are to adults. They are a sign of street cred and command instant respect. Don't make your toddler resort to lies about boo-boos just to get a few. Ten or twenty must be worn at all times, preferably on the arms and face, where other toddlers can see them. A toddler who walks out of the house wearing no Band-Aids hasn't been anywhere or seen anything.

The healing properties of Band-Aids have been documented by magicians. Your toddler cannot get a boo-boo on a part of her body that is covered by a Band-Aid. Had Band-Aids been invented before he was a toddler, Einstein himself would have worn a plastic flesh-toned shield at all times. Some say Band-Aids are essential to life. I'm not an extremist and don't go that far, but I will say they are essential to living.

In conclusion, let me ask you a quick question: Do you love freedom? How do you feel about liberty? When you try to dress your toddler like a chubby mini-hipster to fit some Pinterest vision board, you are on the same level as a flag burner. Not even kidding. You just burned a flag. The flag that waves in your baby's heart.

Parading your toddler around the grocery store in fitted corduroys and a beret means you're not quite ready to be a parent. If your toddler wants to wear last year's Halloween costume to church, let her be. Your two-year-old needs to wear a cowboy hat, rain boots, and a swimsuit to day care? Who cares. And who says pajamas aren't wedding attire? This attachment to social constructs is probably why you're tired all the time.

Homework: Gather up all the washcloths, toothbrushes, and assorted soaps in your home. Throw them in the outside trash. Buy Band-Aids in bulk. Tell your friends.

A Note About Housework

This may shock you, but toddlers love helping. Pick your jaw up off the floor, it's true. Contributing to the work flow of the household gives little (but powerful!) ones an increased sense of importance. Young children are often reluctant to overextend their generous spirits due to a fear that their good nature will be taken advantage of. One minute you're making a thoughtful gesture, like picking up the playroom; the next minute you're a 2T unpaid butler living under the stairs. Below is a guide for allowing your toddler to help around the house on his terms.

Dishes

Toddlers love to help with the dishes. No, we won't scrape off food debris, rinse them, or put away clean ones. Unloading an entire dishwasher is a task beyond most toddlers' skill set. We love sitting sinkside and assisting with bubble migration. You may need to hold your child while going about your dish business. Not with two hands, of course—you have work to do—a simple one-handed secure perch is fine. You'll know when your child is ready for a dishes management position if she's crying at your feet while you stand at the sink. Think of it as an official inquiry.

Sweeping

Nothing says fun time like a broom, but keep in mind that your toddler's objectives where sweeping is concerned may be a little different from yours. Much like squirrels, tots like to burrow and hide food around their natural habitats. It is easy to mistake these strongholds of provisions for rubbish. While you sweep up, your toddler will, in a state of panic, inspect your accumulations for valuables. These treasures include but are not limited to: Cheerios, dust bunnies in fun shapes, Cheetos dust, and coins. It may seem insulting to have someone many years your junior double-check your work, but there's no "I" in "humility." Even if there were, who cares. If you paid as much attention to your sweeping as you did my spelling, you wouldn't need so much help.

Spraying and Wiping

Give a toddler a rag and a spray bottle, and your house will be sparkling before you know it. First it will be soaking, and your mobile phone may have water damage, but after a thorough wipe-down, the results will please you. If you have a policy against cleaning electrical outlets, let your child know ahead of time.

Laundry

Finally got around to that laundry pile? Good for you. Toddlers love this game. How it works: You create a tower of folded shirts. Baby Godzilla knocks it down and blows you away with her strength and agility. Try not to weep from being so impressed. Repeat indefinitely. Pretend to get upset, if you like to spice things up. Need another activity? That basket of yours isn't just for socks. Show your toddler how much you care by taking him on a crazy train ride through the house. If you're too busy, I guess a questionable stranger off the street can do it.

Dear HT,

Sometimes I want to watch something on television, but my toddler insists on monopolizing the TV with the same episode of *Clifford* she saw earlier in the day. It doesn't seem fair. Can I love my toddler and get my way at the same time?

—Struggling on the West Coast

Dear Struggling,

I'm so glad you brought this up. No. You can't love your toddler and think about your own needs at the same time. Have a wonderful day and enjoy *Clifford*.

xo, HT

8

Books, Television, and Games: Understanding and Spending Real Money on Toddler Entertainment .

Toddler life may seem simple from the outside, but if you're not wearing 2T pants, you probably have no idea what you're doing. From television shows to park etiquette, toddler life is rich with ritual and hidden meanings. Proceed with caution.

Daily Schedule

Days are long. Some of them can last twenty hours or more. To make sure your toddler doesn't regret making his way through the birth canal, consider a schedule. Don't write it in pen, as events are subject to change without notice. Below is my personal daily schedule, for inspiration purposes.

4:45 A.M. Wake up. Work on my memoirs.
5 A.M. Alert the parental units.
5:01 A.M. Notice that no one has come. Escalate.
5:01:30 A.M. Hear parental whispering over whose job it is to

fetch me turning into a disagreement over which is harder, working inside or outside of the home.

5:02 A.M. Hear Mommy say, "I'd like to see you try it for one day."

5:02:30 A.M. Hear Daddy say, "I didn't sleep last night, either."

5:03 A.M. Daddy comes in. Don't hide my disappointment.

5:04 A.M. Crackers and milk in between my parents as they fade in and out of fitful sleep. Giggles.

7 A.M. Second breakfast. Eat next to nothing (to stay nimble).

8 A.M. to 9:50 A.M. Tomfoolery.

9:50 A.M. Prenap hysterics. Break something.

10 A.M. Nap.

Noon Reject lunch.

12:30 P.M. Ask for lunch.

12:30:30 P.M. Shame the woman for eating my lunch.

12:40 P.M. Lunch.

12:40 P.M. to 3 P.M. Think about Daddy.

3 P.M. to 5:30 P.M. UP, while crying.

5:30 P.M. Greet my soul mate.

5:30 to 6 P.M. Gleefully play.

6 to 8 P.M. Fight the power.

8 P.M. Go to bed.

8 P.M. to 5 A.M. Shenanigans.

Television

Television shows are best watched from five A.M. to seven P.M. Any less and your toddler may miss something. While there are a variety of shows your toddler will love, she's guaranteed to have her favorites, which will need to be watched in a loop.

Max and Ruby

This is a crime drama based on the hit book and movie *Misery*. In this animated series, a controlling and abusive female rabbit holds her younger brother captive. She often makes him serve as both slave and entertainment for her guests, and believes every day is her birthday. Max appears to be under the influence of mind-control drugs. Their parents are not present, as it seems Ruby *took care* of them.

Sesame Street

A comedy series featuring mutant celebrities. Those skits often push an educational agenda but are entertaining nonetheless. While the cast is all smiles while the cameras are rolling, tensions behind the scenes have caused problems in recent years. After Elmo, the show's four-year-old bear/monster, known for having the voice of an elf, was given his own world, a rivalry was sparked between him and the pterodactyl Big Bird. Producers' efforts to rein in the Shaq vs. Kobe–esque conflict have been unsuccessful. Sponsors are alphabetical in nature.

Dora the Explorer

An ongoing documentary about a poorly supervised young girl with a wild imagination (liar) who is just trying to find her way home. Unfortunately, her map is enchanted, so she never will.

Caillou

This fool. This. fool. I don't even know what to say.

Wonder Pets!

If I'm ever in a dangerous predicament, feel free to call 911. While the concept of a sneaker-wearing turtle, a duckling, and a guinea pig coming to the rescue is adorable, the fact that they admit they're not "too big" or "too tough" leaves me uneasy. Why are they bragging? Someone has to graduate at the bottom of the class, but you don't need to advertise it.

Still, this ragtag team of animal misfits has done a lot right when it comes to launching a small business. I doubt they've filed incorporation papers (silly, in such a highly litigious field), but as evidenced by that corded landline/pencil holder, they are making an effort to keep the overhead low.

Games Without Tears

Awww, your childhood is over. How sad. One way to improve your life is to increase your toddler's happiness. Let's play a game! To make this experience more enjoyable (for toddlers), I've generously put together a brief guideline, if you will. And you will.

Warm-up (pregame). Before you start the game of your toddler's choice, ask yourself, "Have we played this before?" If you have, you're going to do it THE EXACT SAME WAY. Hope you remember the rules.

Attire. You can wear whatever allows you to move, run, and jump comfortably. Be sure you've used the bathroom recently, as there will be no breaks. Make sure you've eaten recently, as there will be no breaks. Drink some water, as there will be no breaks.

Cell-phone policy. Do your online friends/enemies need your attention? These people you've never met or very rarely see— are they more important than the child you brought into this world? Unless you're a 911 operator, there is no reason to even glance down at your phone. God help you if you take a call.

Game on. Are you ready for some football! Monday night par-tay! LOL, you're not playing football. Or traditional hide-and-seek (more on that soon). The game you're playing is far more complicated but, interestingly enough, less structured. There are strict regulations that can change at a moment's notice, so it's vital that you pay attention and watch your kid for cues.

He might guide your face, hands, arms, or legs during the game to let you know what to do. If you're playing Human Slide on the bed (you're the slide, your kid is the happy child), you need to keep your legs straight while your toddler makes his way down. Since you have adult muscles, be strong and don't complain. Nothing hurts.

If you're playing Under the Blanket Tent, also on the bed, remember not to be greedy with the oxygen, as your kid will need some, too. If you feel yourself getting hot, uncomfortable, or short of breath, slow your air intake. Ask yourself if you love your toddler.

Disobedience. Was there an instruction that you didn't understand because you weren't listening properly? Please don't use excuses like "That's impossible" or "What are you saying?"

Laughing. If you hear giggling, congrats! You're on the right track. Repeat whatever you just did until sunset.

Postgame. This is a trick. Game never ends. LOL.

Important Note: You can wear whatever you want, but your toddler will be nude. Depending on his or her state of cleanliness, you may notice some odors. Please don't make a big deal. Also, there is a chance that during the game, your sweet baby may pee in excitement or fury. This is not a reason to end the game. That is what towels were invented for.

Hide-and-Seek

This game originated from fugitives but has gone mainstream. It will have your toddler giggling for hours if you do it right.

Step 1: Close your eyes and count to ten.
Step 2: Open your eyes and notice your toddler standing in front of you, staring.
Step 3: Tell your toddler to go hide.
Step 4: Close your eyes and count to ten slower than you ever have before.
Step 5: Open your eyes and notice that your toddler is crouching at your feet.

Step 6: Gently instruct your toddler to hide in another room.

Step 7: Close your eyes and count to fifteen.

Step 8: Open your eyes and wander from room to room as your toddler laughs hysterically from behind the couch.

Step 9: Wonder aloud where your toddler is.

Step 10: When your toddler jumps out from his hiding place, accept defeat and serve cookies on any old plate.

Hiding

Not to be confused with hide-and-seek, hiding is a special game that toddlers play alone. Are you on your third set of house keys? Missing a remote control? Keep looking while your toddler follows innocently behind you, doing absolutely nothing at all. Maybe it's behind the couch? In the trash? Try asking your toddler. You'll get either a cryptic answer, such as "Gone," or a blank stare. Bribes won't work. Neither will threats, so cool it. Just keep searching. Turn the house upside down. Have you looked under the bed? You're so cute.

Books

Books are wonderful entertainment, gum, and weapons. Many parents read whole stories and don't skip pages, but I wouldn't know anything about that. When you're done texting, take a moment to learn about toddler favorites.

The Giving Tree

Don't be confused by the title. This book is about taking—more specifically, taking everything you can and then taking a bit more just to be safe.

In this book, a young boy with beautiful overalls kills a tree over the course of many years.

I love this story because it shows me that everything is mine, just like I thought. "Reach for the stars," this book says. "Hit them out of the sky with a stick."

Blueberries for Sal

Oh, I love this book.

It's a heartwarming tale about a kid tragically named Sal. After Sal and her mother lose everything, they are forced to steal fruit from nature. Like all gifted children, Sal cannot control her behavior and almost gets herself and her mother killed by bears. This does not change how Santa feels about Sal, or how many presents she will receive, because forgiveness is the key.

My favorite part is where Sal steals food and nobody yells. Imagine that.

The Very Hungry Caterpillar

This is a book about an insect that will soon be dead because it has no instincts. It's a very sad story, so don't read it at night or if you're alone. The moral of the story is to not eat people food unless you're a people. Should go without saying. Enjoy the lifelike photos in this horrible tale. The book will melt if you give it a bath, so keep your receipt.

Love You Forever

This book is about a mother who uses magic to keep her son dependent on her for life. Whenever he starts showing signs of readiness to leave the home, she uses the following spell to kill his spirit and put him into a trance: "I'll love you forever / I'll love you for always / As long as I'm living / My baby you'll be."

The School of Hogwarts has publicly spoken out against this mother's actions.

Are You My Mother?

Have you ever met a fool face-to-face? You're about to. In this hilarious tale, a baby bird traces his roots all the way to a dog and a truck. I know. While he'll never amount to anything, I enjoyed watching him make mistake after mistake. It really says something that the mother bird never came looking for him.

If You Give a Mouse a Cookie

Ever wonder what happens when you don't set limits for rodents? I didn't, either, until I heard this story. Now I have another irrational fear. Thanks for that.

I didn't know mice were so greedy. This book has caused me to second-guess my friendship with Mickey. We're not talking until I figure some things out. This book took away my ability to trust.

The Cat in the Hat

This story has one simple lesson: Babysitters can't be trusted. When a mother chooses errands over her two small children, a nanny whom I can describe only as a cat/man hybrid introduces them to drugs. The caregiver with no references ransacks their home looking for valuables and even invites over his shady friends. I was too scared to finish this book.

Harold and the Purple Crayon

Delinquent baby Harold somehow removes his ankle monitor and escapes house arrest one night. He spends the evening tagging the whole town with graffiti. It's too late for this child; without a doubt, he will soon be back in jail. Lesson: Infants are bad people.

Brown Bear, Brown Bear, What Do You See?

If the idea of animals sharing what's in their direct line of vision is exciting to you, you'll love this book. Whoever wrote it was out of ideas and knew nothing about wildlife. You're going to tell me that a bear, duck, horse, dog, cat, goldfish, and sheep are all within walking distance and living in harmony? I'd be lying if I said this book didn't make me angry.

Movies
(with star ratings)

The Velveteen Rabbit

This isn't so much a film as it is a threat. A young boy gets sick and is punished by having to watch his toys burn. Basically, adults are sending a message: If you inconvenience them with illness, say goodbye to your personal belongings. At the end, there's something about a rabbit, but I missed that part.*

Bambi

A young deer and his mom are enjoying wildlife when there is an explosion. The force of the blast stresses out the mother deer, so she goes to sleep. Moms are always looking for an excuse to lie down, so that part really hit home for me. While the mom relaxes, the baby deer plays with his father. They do hood-rat stuff for the next ten years or so.***

Aladdin

This movie is about life in the Middle East. I don't normally enjoy documentaries, but this one wasn't half bad. My favorite part was seeing Rajah, the enslaved tiger, finally turn on her master. This part happened only in my imagination. All the sand will make you thirsty, so be sure to have three or four juice boxes within reach.*****

Charlotte's Web

When a pig escapes a bacon transformation by showing signs of literacy, the whole town loses its mind. Turns out the pig doesn't have any special skills and was riding the coattails of a tarantula. I don't get it, either.**

Pinocchio

This is another passive-aggressive movie invented by adults to shape children's behavior. The subliminal message is clear: If you lie, your body will get deformed. I know this isn't true because I lie all the time and look great. It's ironic that there's a lie in a movie about not lying. Younger toddlers may fall for this foolishness. Zero out of five stars for the hypocrisy.

The Red Balloon

We've all been there. A restaurant employee or grocery store clerk gives you a balloon, and five minutes later, it's heading toward the sun. Unfortunately, this child is so poorly supervised that, rather than just cry for the rest of the day, he chases his balloon around Paris. I admire his ambition but fear that he never found his way home and had to live on the streets.***

Mary Poppins

This movie confirmed everything I know to be true about babysitters: They're full of tricks. I'm not sure if this lady is being paid to sing, but she sure does a lot of it. She uses the forces of the underworld liberally.*

Cinderella

You can't trust people just because they're family. I feel so sorry for this girl, but I love how she takes her revenge in the end. Her relationship to rodents is inspiring. I wasn't surprised when her fairy grandmother saved the day, because my own grandma has rescued me from difficult situations on several occasions.*****

The Sound of Music

This romantic comedy isn't for children. It features seven siblings dressed from head to toe in Goodwill. When a negligent babysitter comes into these kids' lives, they have no choice but to scare her off. She abandons her post midshift and steals a guitar on her way out. Several days later, she returns; and instead of being dismissed on the spot, nanny is promoted to mommy. At the end, the family takes up residence in the nearby mountains to prepare for *American Idol* auditions.*

The Wizard of Oz

The lesson is crystal-clear in this one: Don't fall asleep. Zero out of five stars.

Music

All toddlers love music, whether it's the sound of their own crying or noise from a traditional radio. Here's a guide to what's keeping toddler toes tapping in their Crocs.

"Eensy-Weensy Spider"

This isn't a song for everyone, as it's about the reincarnation of an arachnid.

"Old MacDonald"

This song should be illegal under current child-labor laws. This farmer needs to start doing his own inventory rather than depending on toddlers. Keep track of your animals, Mr. MacDonald. We're done doing your dirty work.

"Frère Jacques"

I have no idea what this song is about, but it's catchy.

"You Are My Sunshine"

I like this song, but don't call someone your sunshine your only sunshine and then hug Daddy five seconds later.

"Row Your Boat"

This is an eerie but comforting song about a ship. Don't expect more.

Fairy-Tale Reviews

Hansel and Gretel

When a couple of parents find themselves struggling to make ends meet, their first and only idea is to abandon their two young children in the woods. Don't turn to family for help. Don't start your own marketing business selling candles to reluctant friends. Don't switch to generic brands. Why cut back on expenses or consolidate debt when you can just get rid of your dependents? Despite this troubling and irresponsible premise, Hansel and Gretel is a classic among parents looking for an easy way out.

If you're at all tempted to solve your financial problems by deserting your toddler, keep reading. It should be no surprise to anyone that Hansel and his sister, Gretel, turned to a life of crime shortly after being left to fend for themselves. Their first offense was to vandalize the home of a nearby witch. She was forced to keep them in her custody until the authorities arrived, but the children killed her first. Neither the brother nor the sister in this crime partnership has ever been brought before the law, and if you see them on the street, assume they are armed and dangerous.

Lesson: Wood chopping is not a real profession. It will leave your family destitute. That said, a lack of funds is no excuse for giving up your children. It's called a small-business loan.

Snow White and the Seven Dwarfs

Snow White is an overwhelmed mother and aspiring model. No one made her have seven children, but that won't stop her from complaining to anyone who will listen. Being "the most beautiful of them all" is her number one preoccupation. While most single mothers are known for being hardworking and self-sacrificing, Snow White sends her children into the mines to search for precious metals while she takes an e-course on eyebrow threading.

When a rival model moves to town, Snow White loses it; she

can't think clearly because she's been dieting her whole life. Her nemesis sends a gift that she thinks Snow White will appreciate—an apple: low-calorie, low-sugar, nonfat. Snow White suspiciously accepts the gift, but after one bite, her blood sugar spikes, and having been depleted for so long, she passes out for months. I didn't understand the rest of the story.

Lesson: Do not let vanity get in the way of being the best parent you can be. Your toddler doesn't care if you're dirty and unshaven. Actually, he probably prefers it.

Humpty Dumpty

This fool doesn't know he's made out of eggshell material, and climbs to epic heights. His inevitable fall is the talk of the century. Egg yolk and whites go everywhere, and his community rushes to collect it for the biggest omelet ever made. There are no vegetables or designer cheeses in the omelet, so the neighborhood toddlers are free to enjoy. Humpty Dumpty left a delicious legacy that is still talked about today.

Lesson: Humpty Dumpty was made of eggshell, but your toddler isn't. Let her climb as high as she wants, and don't make a big deal.

Goldilocks and the Three Bears

This is one of my favorite fairy tales. I only wish more parents would pay attention to the messages in the story rather than getting caught up in the details. Goldilocks was born in the San Fernando Valley, an area in California known for very little. Twenty years ago, she wandered into a tract home occupied by a bear family. Goldilocks had been casing the house for months, and the minute it seemed like the bear family would be gone for a few hours, she descended.

After jimmying the locks, she began to ransack the home for valuables: Gold, silver, electronics, she took them all. Just as she was on her way out, she noticed food on the table. Since she'd eaten nothing but Arby's for weeks, a home-cooked meal was irresistible. Through trial and error, she figured out which bowl of porridge was at the right temperature. The meal was a trap. It contained sedatives that left her dizzy and looking for a comfortable place to lie down. On her way upstairs, she broke three chairs.

It was then that the bears sprang into the home with a camera crew and surprised Goldilocks. Turns out she's Papa Bear's niece, and this was her official intervention. Her whole family flooded the room, where a confused and humiliated Goldilocks was confronted with her fast-paced lifestyle and given the opportunity to change.

Lesson: Who makes porridge? Is this 1913? Gross. Cook normal foods. You're not cute.

Rumpelstiltskin

This story became popular when gold prices started going up. Parents loved the idea of using their children to create wealth.

The tale begins with a father and his young daughter. Lots of parents brag, but this father didn't know where facts ended and reality began. When he noticed that many of his friends had talented children who could throw balls far, and remember long strings of numbers, he decided to one-up them with a doozy of a lie. He told everyone that his daughter could turn straw into gold. The king of his village got word and kidnapped the girl. He told her that if she turned a room of straw into gold, she would live to see the next day. The girl's father noticed her missing but failed to issue an AMBER Alert.

Knowing that she did not possess the gift of alchemy, the girl was distraught. Out of nowhere, a large bedbug named Rumpelstiltskin popped up and made her a proposition: If he turned all the straw into gold, she'd reward him with a one-year Netflix membership. She agreed. Rumpelstiltskin worked through the night, and by sunrise, the king had his gold. Being greedy, the king brought her to an even bigger room of straw and demanded results. Again, Rumpelstiltskin came to the rescue. In return for another miracle, the girl would have to give him an iPad. She was reluctant but agreed, and by dawn, yet another room of gold had been created.

This is where the story gets crazy. The king demanded one last room of gold and promised to marry his captive if she delivered. *What a deal.* By this point, the lady had Stockholm syndrome and identified strongly with her kidnapper. She couldn't wait to hear wedding bells and go on *Say Yes to the Dress,* so she called on Rumpelstiltskin again. He made a wild demand: If she would give him her firstborn child, she'd have one final room of gold. Not knowing that wrinkled infants sometimes turn into beautiful toddlers, she agreed. Two years, a very expensive televised wedding, and one baby later, Rumpelstiltskin arrived to pick up his kid. The new mom refused, and when Rumpelstiltskin began to have a loud response, she had him thrown from the roof.

Lesson: Verbal contracts mean nothing. Also, don't brag about your kids. Nobody cares.

Sleeping Beauty

This fairy tale is about naps and how easily they can get out of control. Hundreds of years ago in a faraway kingdom, a princess was born. Her parents invited the paparazzi to the child's first birthday party, hoping to sell the photos. Unfortunately, one of the camerapeople was also a nanny. She overstepped her bounds and put the child down for a nap. Here's the twist: No one was able to wake the girl up! Years went by, and the princess grew, all while sleeping. Potty training was impossible. Twenty years passed, and the king and queen started to worry that, in her immobilized state, their daughter would never find a prince, so they ordered one online. He'd been snacking on hummus and tzatziki dip on his flight over, and by the time he arrived, his breath was so terrible that it instantly snapped Sleeping Beauty out of her deep sleep.

Lesson: Don't buy weird dips.

Rapunzel

Parents love to confine their children. This is just a fact of life, but that doesn't make it right. It's hard to remember, but your toddler is not some kind of songbird that you can keep locked away. She's more like a wild dog who needs limited supervision and a big yard. The story of Rapunzel will chill you to the core: a tale of a privileged child whose pedigree could not save her from overprotective adults.

Day care, preschool, and primary school have one thing in common: badness. The frightening tale of Rapunzel is evidence. Shortly after her birth, toddler Rapunzel was sent off to a fancy boarding school with a long waiting list in an abandoned tower. Little did her parents know that the institution they chose was a cult, and poor Rapunzel was subjected to hard daily labor. Rather than retrieve her, they held a paper-lantern festival every year. Yes, you heard right, a paper-lantern festival. I know.

Rapunzel was forced to wear her hair hippie-long and eat shiitake mushroom chips; her life was terrible by any toddler standard. Thankfully, as Rapunzel was air-drying her hair out the window one day, an FBI agent climbed up her mane and led a raid on the school. Rapunzel's first act of freedom was to give herself a bob. She's still very active in human rights.

Lesson: Fancy preschools aren't always what they're cracked up to be. Skip education.

The Emperor's New Clothes

Basically, a toddler king decides he wants naked time, so he goes for it.

Lesson: Just because you don't love your body doesn't mean your toddler can't love his. Toddlers know how glorious their forms are, and aren't afraid to flaunt what their mamas gave them, even if their mamas are chasing them through the park, clutching their pants.

Toys

Thankfully, there are millions of toys on the market. However, getting parents to take them from the store induces frustration and vomiting in toddlers. Adults, what exactly is so difficult about sliding a plastic card through the machine? Are you afraid of spraining your wrist? A paper cut from the receipt? No. You're being stubborn, and everyone can see it. If you're confused about which toys to go out and grab, use my official guide.

1. **Puzzles.** Every toddler needs at least three puzzles. Never try to make your toddler do the puzzle himself, as this is impossible. Sit on the floor and do it alone while your toddler watches. Your self-esteem will go through the roof. Six hours after buying the puzzle, one or all of the pieces will be missing. Don't make a big deal; you had fun while it lasted. Just throw the empty container in the outside trash.

2. **Stuffed animals** (with or without nursery magic). Stuffed animals generally come alive in the night, so stay away from those with menacing dispositions. Bears are good; giraffes are traitors. Your toddler needs a hundred. Not one less. Gold star if you find one over four feet tall to serve as the guardian of your home. Before bed, your toddler will need help arranging and rearranging her animal friends. Just do your job, please. *Private Practice* can wait.

3. **String.**

4. **Your mobile device.** I should actually say "your child's mobile device," because after you're gone, everything will belong to your toddler anyway, right? Don't hog it. Ninety-seven percent of the games on there are for your kid. Like you have anyone to call.

This is just a bare-bones list. You still need to pick up cars, dolls, and other miscellaneous items. When you can't see the floor anymore, you're doing great.

iPad

iPads are mirrors that took things to the next level. If your toddler doesn't have an iPad, she doesn't know what a good time looks or feels like. The best part about iPads is that they let you come as you are. Your hands can be covered with peanut butter or dripping with honey. This toy will just form a smooth, glossy crust out of whatever you bring to the table.

There are hundreds of games to play and contacts to delete. When your toddler clears your address book, he's saying, "You are mine." Open your heart to this message of love, and cut your friends out of your life once and for all. If your songs, movies, or books go missing, see it as a form of censorship by your toddler. You don't have time for books other than this one, let's be honest about that. What are you reading? Nothing. Your music is nonsensical and makes you feel carefree (you're not).

When your toddler asks you to download a new game and you refuse because ninety-nine cents is out of the budget, one can only wonder where you learned to lie so well. You don't have one dollar? We all know your toddler does not have an existing college fund. Perhaps these apps, games, and movies can be your way of making an investment in your child's future. If that pains you too much, don't worry about it. Someone has to fail in life. Why not your child? When your offspring is stealing copper from foreclosed homes twenty years from now, remember this crossroads moment while you cry. It'll be too late, but maybe your story will inspire another family to link a credit card to the iTunes store.

iPads are indestructible, but every now and then, a powerful toddler fails to recognize her own strength. Don't make a big deal. When your toddler kills the iPad, through either juice saturation or a short but fatal flight across the room, just pick it up and bury it in the front yard. The people of Apple will bring a new one in five to seven days; all you have to do is give them hundreds of dollars. What's money when you have love?

Arts and Crafts

Arts and crafts are when you cut something that belongs to someone else. This can be paper, drapes, clothes, hair, or pillows. First get your hands on some scissors. Keep five to six pairs in the house for your toddler. The sharper the better, as shoes are very difficult to cut through.

Art isn't just about destroying. Gluing is a fantastic way for your toddler to express negative or positive feelings.

Unless you like seeing your life's work in the trash, please refrain from throwing away your child's creations. There are few things more painful than peeking into the recycling bin and seeing one of your murals. Try to wrap your mind around what that does to a young spirit.

Paired with a purple-drink juice box or a mild string cheese, Play-Doh will also delight your toddler's senses. For a richer experience, please open up your wallet and buy more than three colors at a time. Left overnight to marinate in air, Play-Doh will take on a delicate crispy texture. Getting hungry just thinking about it.

Friends

In the adult world, one of the most common misconceptions about toddlers is that we make friendships based on height. No, not all toddlers are friends. The process of choosing one's inner circle is long and rigorous. Toddlers choose friends based on the following criteria.

1. **Snack quality:** Nobody wants to be buddies with a kid whose fridge is bursting at the seams with garlic paste. It's just not going to happen. If you want your child to have comrades, learn where your local grocery store keeps the shredded cheese.
2. **Television policy:** Don't own a TV? Good for you! Enjoy being your kid's best friend for life.

3. **Toys:** Your rustic wooden blocks may be perfect for Instagram photos, but you're raising a loner if you don't get at least one toy that requires batteries. Truth.

Once your home is snack, show, and toy ready, set up a playdate. "What is a playdate?" you're asking yourself. Great question.

A playdate is:
1. A fantastic way to break out of a stale routine.
2. An opportunity for your toddler to show another toddler his toys. Show. For eyes. Notice the lack of touching of what doesn't belong to you.
3. A chance for your child to sample snacks that you don't currently have in your home.

A playdate is not:
1. The time for you to chitchat with an old friend about the latest prime-time series.
2. Happy hour.

Parents, do not try to impress your guest's caregivers with your child's sharing abilities if they do not exist. Surprise—this isn't about you.

Running

The number one game among all toddlers is running without a destination, which is obviously best done nude, as clothing creates wind resistance. Your toddler will begin running at approximately four-forty-five A.M. and will finish when you abruptly end the game, citing "bedtime" as a reason. Help make running extra-fantastic for your child by clearing your home of furniture and walls.

While running, your toddler may release energy by screaming.

The run/scream combo will fill your home with peace. Not "peace and quiet," the other kind. Look it up.

"Calm down." Have you said this today? Hopefully, you didn't mean it. I'm not sure what "calm down" means, exactly, but I think it's how lethargic adults tell spirited toddlers to voluntarily give up some of their life force. Read that sentence again and ask yourself if what you want is for your toddler to calm down or instead for you to power UP. Don't try to deny it. I see all those empty Red Bulls and 5-hour ENERGY drinks. You wish you had half your toddler's stamina. Jealousy looks bad on you. Really bad. Years of grilled vegetables have left you weak, and there's nothing you can do about it. Accept. Move on. Try to stay awake.

- -

Homework: Visit the toy store and get all the things. Next, go to a field. Run until nightfall.

- -

Dear Honest Toddler,

My two-and-a-half-year-old believes that every day is his birthday. Help.

—Lost in Ontario

Dear Lost,

I know Ontario is a province in Canada, but other than that, I cannot help you, because I don't know where you're trying to go. How did you end up there? Were you blindfolded on the journey? Hope you find your way back soon. Happy birthday to your little boy.

xo, HT

Special Occasions: Making Them Magical for Your Sweet Angel

It seems as though, every few weeks, there is something to celebrate. Whether it is a real holiday, like my birthday, or a fake one, like Thanksgiving, the most important thing to remember is that it is your responsibility to make the day magical. If there is no cake, consider yourself a failure.

Birthdays

I woke up sensing something in the air. She wasn't pushing her feet like dogs refusing to be walked—no—I could hear her practically skipping around the kitchen, like in the opening scene of Cinderella. *You know, the one where the fatherless future princess wakes up in rags and is subsequently groomed and dressed by a team of woodland creatures. The circular clinking of the spoon in her coffee was faster than usual. She's awake before me? And seems alert. How is this possible? Even with the haze of sleep still weighing heavy on my small form, I could sense her excitement.*

My footie pajamas couldn't protect me from a wave of cold dread that quickly spread through my entire body. "She's finally done it," I thought. "She put me on eBay, like she's threatened so many times before, and my buyers are coming to collect me." Why else would she be whistling? I let out a cry. Within moments, both parents were crib-side, grinning. "Happy birthday!"

In seconds I went from potentially losing the only home I'd ever known to being crowned like royalty. It may have been cardboard adorned with plastic jewels, but to me, it was the first step of many toward taking my rightful place as the ruler of everything. Balloons were placed in almost every corner of our home, a large table with a plastic tablecloth featuring my favorite television friends was erected outside, with heaping bowls of chips, platters of fresh gleaming fruit. I felt as if in a dream. Then the doorbell rang . . .

HAPPY BIRTHDAY TO *ME*

There seems to be a lot of confusion concerning what qualifies as an appropriate birthday party. A gathering of freeloading stranger babies is not a celebration. You may love sharing your special day, toys, cake, and attention with acquaintances, but chances are, the toddler in your life would rather watch a Lifetime original-movie marathon.

Below is a handy guide for planning a fête (that's Russian) that your toddler will surely be somewhat thankful for.

Birthday-Party Requirements

1. **Cake:** First, calm down. There is nothing wrong with sugar. It is a vitamin and a source of hydration. If your toddler has a legitimate allergy—confirmed with a note from a medical professional rather than a hunch—you may substitute sugar, wheat, dairy, or eggs with caramel. Choosing a "special" allergy cake for the sake of a child attendee is ridiculous. Whose birthday is it again? That's what I thought.

A party isn't a party without cake, so make sure you choose the right one. Fruit in the shape of a cake is not cake. Banana bread (OMG) is not cake. Real cake comes from the grocery store or the bakery. Just keep an eye out for the cake smell. If you love your toddler, decorate the cake with heroes and designs. Throw on a few Skittles and candy bars to make it especially fantastic. Sprinkle five to six cups of powdered sugar, aka heaven's snow, if being magnificent means anything to you.

You're probably asking yourself, "When is the right time to present my toddler with her birthday cake?" The first mistake you made was asking the question. The best time to serve the cake is when your toddler remembers it exists.

A common but terrible custom that has become popular due to peer pressure is the cutting and sharing of a toddler's birthday cake. Wow. Way to make assumptions. Legally, the cake belongs to the person being celebrated, so when you slice it up and pass out pieces, you are distributing stolen goods and deserve whatever happens to you. An alternate tradition that is becoming quite trendy is the practice of allowing partygoers to watch your toddler eat the whole cake. People greatly enjoy sitting around a table admiring the birthday child as she takes bite after delicious bite. It's okay to clap.

Leftover pieces of cake should be stored on the bottom shelf of the fridge in a Tupperware with no lid.

2. **Invitations:** Invitations are unnecessary, as this isn't a wedding. Most likely, your toddler does not want friends or family at the birthday party. Other children are especially unwelcome.

3. **Goody Bags:** What a fabulous idea. Give people who aren't the birthday boy or girl a gift on the way out. After you've distributed all the goody bags, be sure to drape a blanket over your toddler, as he has probably fainted from devastation.

Creating goody bags for kids who have not earned or paid for them is a waste of family resources and a personal betrayal.

Throwing the Ideal Birthday Party

Taking direction can be difficult (trust me, I know), so below you'll find a description of the perfect birthday party. Please use this narrative as motivation to create something truly spectacular for your child.

Toddler wakes up just before dawn and is immediately attended to, without sad faces. Parents take turns hugging their sweet baby for thirty to forty-five minutes. They whisper, "Happy birthday, amazing child!" over and over.

Breakfast: sprinkles with butter. A classic favorite. And look—there are birthday candles in the butter! Toddler blows out all eighteen candles with ease, power, and grace. The whole world erupts in thunderous applause and then apologizes profusely for being so loud.

Toddler leaves the kitchen table and is immediately handed a Ziploc bag full of trail mix (chocolate chips, gummy vitamins, and cereal puffs). Time to nakedly watch TV shows.

Four hours later, it's birthday-party time! No one arrives. There are wrapped gifts everywhere and extra wrapping paper for ripping. Parents walk into the room carrying a large cake. It's so heavy that they can barely hold it, but they don't dare drop it on the floor, because their hearts are full of love. Toddler blows out the forty-eight candles, then eats handful after handful of cake.

It's time to open presents. Wow! A bike! Amazing! Unlimited Play-Doh! Fantastic! A pocketknife! Toddler is too busy playing to say "thank you," but no one makes a big deal.

Toddler is so excited that some pee-pee comes out. It is cleaned up quickly and quietly.

Time for goody bags! They are all handed to toddler.

At eleven-forty-five P.M., toddler falls asleep in the big bed, ready to do it all again tomorrow.

Now that you know how to throw a birthday bash for your toddler, you're out of excuses. Follow these instructions, and remember, it's not about you. It never was.

Christmas

Once every eighteen months, a benevolent recluse holds the world hostage with promises of gifts. We call this man Santa. Despite being accused of using elf labor in slumlord-esque working conditions, Santa is celebrated for bringing peace and Ferrero Rocher to the world. Parents, you have one job during Christmastime: Don't mess it up.

It is not your job to use lies and false reporting to destroy the relationship your child has developed with Santa. Nor is it appropriate to manipulate your toddler's behavior with threats. I've had the privilege of speaking with a North Pole representative who has assured me that Santa is NOT concerned with who finishes his or her vegetables. You must feel so silly right now. Like Santa ever cared about zucchini when he himself lives on candy canes and donated cookies. Santa also said that he doesn't personally know you. So all that talk of "Don't make me get on the phone with Santa"? How do you live with yourself? Seriously. How do you look in the mirror and feel good when every other word you say is a lie? I want to know. If you've already clouded Santa's opinion of your child, please send him the following letter to make things right.

> *Dear Santa,*
>
> *This is _____'s [insert name of child]_____ [mom or dad]. I'm writing to let you know that I've been naughty. Despite my years of education and life experience, I still haven't learned to mind my own business. Everything I told you about ____ has been a lie. I just wanted attention.*
>
> *_____ has been excellent this year. Nobody is perfect, but _____ is close. I credit _____ for making me the person I am today. I get plenty of sleep. Nothing is broken in my home.*
>
> *_____ is excellent at sharing and loves going to bed. We don't have problems. What I said before was a result of jealousy and*

insolence on my part. I don't know what's wrong with me, but I'm going to find out.

Attached is _____'s wish list. It is my official recommendation that you give _____ everything ___ [he/she] has asked for, plus a few bonus gifts for being such a wonderful toddler. Some candy wouldn't hurt, either.

Again, I'm sorry for lying. Feel free to give me nothing.

Love, _____ [your name]

It's not all your fault. Much of the fear propaganda that plagues Santa was created by a disgruntled former elf named Dewdrop (street name "Drizzle"). After he was fired for swapping out legitimate gifts for his latest albums, Drizzle the Elf made it his mission to get revenge on Father Christmas. He wrote and produced the popular song "Santa Claus Is Coming to Town," in which St. Nick is portrayed as both a member of Homeland Security and an everyday peeping Tom. The track went platinum and has been played on a loop in Starbucks cafes from November 26 through January 1 ever since. The emotional toll these lyrics have had on children has been serious. These days a kid can't even cry without thinking that he's on a closed-circuit television feed directly to the North Pole.

When I reached out to Dewdrop/Drizzle for comment, he simply said, "All that glitters isn't powdered sugar." No word on what that means.

Once you've stopped using Santa in threats, making Christmas a day for your toddler to remember will be easy. Commit the following steps to memory. I'd say don't wait until the last minute, but we both know you will.

1. **Buy or steal a tree.** Find a big one. If it has birds, violently shake them out. Santa is passionate about nature and loves seeing it indoors. Decorate the tree with glass.
2. **Help your toddler write a list of demands for Santa.**

3. **Get a chimney.** If you live in a condo or an apartment, do not expect any gifts unless you make arrangements ahead of time. Santa doesn't like to think on his feet.

4. **Put out the fire in your fireplace** before bed. Trying to kill Santa, are you? Please get help before you ruin the holiday for everyone.

5. **Leave cookies.** Santa doesn't want your almond-flour stevia abominations, okay? Be normal.

6. **Put out a treat for the reindeer.** Trash works. Food scraps. They're not picky.

We've already touched on the notorious and unstoppable folly of adults. This leads many of them to rationalize hiring fake Santas to interrogate children in malls across the country. Dressing your toddler in red and forcing her to sit with one of these lost souls is like taking the magic of Christmas and cutting it into asymmetrical shapes. Your toddler will provide you with auditory and visual clues, such as going ape-crazy and/or running for her life, to let you know that she's not impressed. Paying twenty-five dollars to have your child's photo taken with a celebrity impersonator shows poor judgment and weak money-management skills. If you're set on having your child meet Santa, charter a jet and visit the North Pole. I guess it's true what they say about common sense not being that common.

Oh, and just because Mr. Claus will be showering your sweetheart with a bounty of toys doesn't mean you can't hit up your local Toys"R"Us and show your toddler how much you appreciate him. Your gifts may not be as good as Santa's, but don't get discouraged. Just do your best. Aim for between eighteen and twenty-five presents and about a hundred small tokens of love for the stocking. Or you can just ride Santa's wave on Christmas morning, if that's the level of excellence you're currently capable of.

On this holiday, let's be inspired by the story of Rudolph. This half goat/half dog couldn't get it right until he embraced his shortcomings. It was only then that he became a shining star and found a way to serve. You, too, can be a Rudolph, guiding your child's proverbial sleigh, if you'd only humble yourself.

Out-of-the-Box Holiday Gift Guide

Don't be fooled by the toy industry. Not all presents need to have bright colors and moving parts (although most should). Take a gander at the following gift ideas, and get to shopping!

Tape

Wow the special toddler in your life with a three-pack of Scotch tape to use at her discretion. You can find tape in most drugstores or office-supply stores. These invisible stickers will give your child hours of clean fun. One of the most exciting parts about a tape gift is that you get to participate. Enjoy helping your toddler remove the tape from his eyebrows. No judgment, please.

Refrigerator Boxes

Or, as we in the toddler world like to call them, "potentiality cubes." If you already have a refrigerator but didn't keep the box, you can easily buy another one at a Sears near you. Once it arrives, throw the fridge away. Bring the box into your home, cut a door in it, and watch as your toddler has the time of his life. Most refrigerators retail at about four hundred to three thousand dollars, but the boxes are all the same.

Scissors

Buy real scissors with the metal blades, not the plastic safety kind that break when you try to cut paper. Scissors help improve hand-eye coordination and confidence. Look around and you'll see signs of your toddler starting to get mentally stronger; all sorts of items in your home and maybe on your person will be permanently altered after your toddler gets done with them. If hairstyles mean something to you, you may want to take your family portraits before presenting this gift.

Spray Bottle Filled with Water

Break a five-dollar bill on this gift and you won't be disappointed. I mean, you might be a little disappointed that everything in your home is perpetually covered with morning dew, but other than that, you'll be pleased. I mean your toddler will be pleased. You'll be trying to treat the mold growth.

Aluminum-Foil Twin Pack

Tinfoil makes plenty of noise. It also looks like a precious metal. Your toddler will have hours of fun pulling the sheets from the roll and crushing them into balls.

Toothpaste

This is to squeeze out and observe, not for brushing purposes. Any color will do, but blue with flavor beads is ideal.

A Note on Relatives

The holidays are difficult for toddlers due to an influx of strangers coming into the home. These people, who claim to be blood-related, often believe that they deserve affection when nothing could be farther from the truth. Please check ID and credentials before allowing a "relative" into your house. Don't take his or her word for it. If you have the resources, run a complete background check for the safety of the smallest members of your home. A DNA test would not be going too far. Even if these people can prove their significance to the family, by no means should they be allowed to stay overnight, as seeing them at breakfast will upset your child for the rest of the day. Hotels were invented for a reason.

FAQ

Should I give relatives my toddler's room when they're in town for the holidays?

Answer: Sure. And while you're at it, give them the family car and your child's spot in your will.

Should my toddler have to give relatives hugs or offer any visible signs of affection?

Answer: Yes. If you're trying to raise a child with no sense of personal boundaries, force him to hug and kiss people he barely knows.

Thank-you cards. Is it useful to write these and have my toddler include original art?

Answer: Go ahead, but make sure the recipients know that the art is on loan and not for keeps. In the near future, when his work is worth millions, your toddler will need all of the drawings back.

When relatives speak to my toddler, she stares at them blankly. What should I do?

Answer: First, confirm that they're speaking similar languages. Second, confirm that your toddler has no reason to hate this relative. Third, leave it alone.

Hanukkah

Hanukkah is a beautiful holiday that celebrates hope: the hope that every day can be a gift day. For eight nights, children are given large presents with faith in their hearts that this can become a permanent thing. Dare to dream.

Valentine's Day

The best part of being a parent on Valentine's Day is that you don't have to worry about finding a valentine. You already birthed one! In some circles, it's customary to exchange gifts, but since your toddler has no money and no job, don't expect anything.

The official foods of Valentine's Day are:

- Chocolate
- Stickers
- Candy hearts

To make the day a success, stock up on all three.

What makes this holiday so different from Christmas is that it's about love. Three days before Valentine's Day, start reflecting on how your toddler has changed your life. What did you have going for you before your cherub burst onto the scene? Don't say "sleep" or "happiness," because you're not funny. Be serious for once in your life, please. Here's a list if you're having problems.

Ways Your Toddler Has Made Life Better

1. No more money wasted on alarm clocks.
2. Encouragement to refine your previously/currently terrible culinary skills.
3. Stronger arms from holding five bags of groceries and your toddler at the same time.
4. Improved balance from holding five bags of groceries and your toddler at the same time while pushing the empty stroller.
5. No more being lonely while using the bathroom.
6. No more being lonely while taking a shower.
7. No more being lonely anytime!
8. Having someone with whom to share your life and everything you eat or drink from now on.

Look how rich your life is. And whom do you have to thank for this bounty of blessings? Say your child's name aloud. Don't be shy. Gratitude can be uncomfortable at first.

Valentine's Day is best started with chocolate-chip pancakes in the shape of hearts. Maybe your toddler will eat a few; maybe he'll rip them apart. There's more than one way to enjoy a meal. Next is the presentation of the chocolate. As you place each delicious morsel in your toddler's hands, say, "Thank you for making me better."

Now lead your child to the room where the other gifts and balloons are waiting. Sit in a corner (try to become invisible) while your toddler has the time of her life.

Television diamond commercials would have you believe that Valentine's Day has something to do with love and hugs between adults. No. That kind of love actually hurts your toddler. We've covered this.

St. Patrick's Day

Green. This holiday celebrates the color green. Try not to make a big deal, as the other colors are still struggling with that. If a leprechaun enters your home, remember to stay calm and make an example out of it.

Easter

Easter always makes me a little sad. While I love the idea of a four-foot-tall rabbit handing out jelly beans, I hate that he'll never fit in. This bunny has probably lost everyone who ever mattered to him because of his size.

Easter-egg hunts can get very competitive. Don't be alarmed if your child sweeps the leg or jumps over an infant. If you're in charge of a local Easter-egg hunt, don't get literal and hide real eggs. This isn't some kind of hobo potluck; it's an activity for children. Don't see it as an opportunity to clean out your fridge.

Mother's Day

On this special day in November, your sweet baby will crawl into bed with you in the morning and hand you a crudely drawn picture. That's it. I hope you weren't expecting a parade. The most important thing to remember about Mother's Day is that without your toddler, you wouldn't be a mother. It makes sense, therefore, to split whatever gifts you receive 50/50.

Father's Day

Congratulations, Daddy, you have a kid. You'll get the same picture (act surprised) and breakfast in bed. Once Best Buy is open, spend the rest of the day bulking up your toddler's DVD collection.

Halloween

I've learned lots of things from Halloween, but the most important lesson has been: Strangers *do* have candy. All you have to do is ask. On this holiday, children around the world wear costumes and beg from their neighbors. Begging is one of a toddler's special skills, so there's no need to practice at home before the big day. There are many aspects to making Halloween wonderful for your toddler, so put your phone on silent, and let's begin. I said silent, not vibrate. Listening is a great skill.

Costume

Halloween is not an opportunity to impress your friends and humiliate your child. Costumes that are obscure references to pop-culture icons will not be tolerated. If this is what your friends appreciate, maybe you should find some people who like you for you. Most toddlers will want to be a fairy, princess, cowboy, dinosaur, dog, or hero. Notice I did not say Frida Kahlo or Mozart. If nobody can guess what your child is dressed as and your explana-tion is paired with a smug chortle, you have made a mistake.

Halloween Roles

On Halloween, adults divide themselves into two categories: run-ners and distributors. Runners accompany children while they col-lect the goods. Distributors provide candy. It seems that in recent years, product standards have decreased dramatically. Distributors, under no circumstances should you EVER pass out dried fruit on Halloween. This day was created to celebrate high fructose, not the natural sweetness of dates. Keep the raisins to yourself. This isn't a day for groceries. What's next? Cold cuts? Sprouts? Soy milk?

Office supplies are also unacceptable. Stickers are a welcome goody on any other day, but you've had months to prepare for this night. Are you going to start giving out rubber bands and return envelopes? If you've even thought of handing out toothbrushes or pennies, please turn off your porch light and go to bed. You can't be trusted with the simplest of tasks.

Thanksgiving

This food-centric holiday was invented by the grocery industry for profit. Generally, families will invite people over to look at your toddler and eat until they can't remember their social security number. Toddlers are against Thanksgiving because of the food and the strangers. Be an advocate for your child and ban Thanks-giving from your home. It takes attention away from what matters most, and I know you know who that is.

Saturdays

This is a fairly frequent holiday where anything goes. You'll be tempted to stay home and do nothing while your toddler cries at your feet. You may not know this, but the park is always open and free. For your toddler, even the library is better than staring at baseboards while his parents watch the Magic Bullet infomercial. If you sit on the couch like you're an iPhone on a charging dock, it will force your toddler to throw your debit card in the trash again. Motivate yourself to put on people clothes. Don't be scared. They won't feel as comfortable as the pajamas you've had on since forever, but you'll adjust. Try lifting your arm. It won't break. Good. Now give standing a shot. It might be painful to straighten out your back, but you can do it. Okay, now one foot in front of the other. Push through the resistance in your muscles. All those salads are doing wonders for your energy, aren't they? Right. Now find the keys and put your toddler in the car. Drive somewhere fun, even if it makes you want to cry. Wow, look at you. This is called parenting.

Dear Honest Toddler,

How do I teach my toddler to respect my cat's personal space?

—Confused in Rhode Island

Dear Confused,

Personal space? Does your cat pay rent? Did he cosign on your home loan? Does he chip in for utilities? Squatters don't have rights.

Love, HT

◆ ◆ ◆

Dear Honest Toddler,

What should I consider before bringing a pet into our home? We have a three-year-old girl.

—Debating in South Carolina

Dear Debating,

The first thing you need to decide is if you want a real or animated pet. Animated pets will take you on adventures, but real pets will eat your garbage. Good luck.

Love, HT

10

Pets:

Helping Your Toddler

Love Them Tight

Animals are wonderful creatures, and toddlers love them. Do you have one in your home? You are very lucky. I had a cat, but it decided to live somewhere else and jumped out the window. It seemed to be in a hurry. Cat and I had our differences, but overall, we were the best of friends, and he loved me.

I also had two fish. They both died. We could point fingers all day, but the blame game will get us nowhere. The most important thing is that no one was hurt. Except the fish. They're dead.

You may have told your toddler that pets are not toys. This is not true. The trick is to be careful. It's time to learn about animals, what makes them tick, and how to take gentle but aggressive care of them.

Cats

What is a cat? A cat is a tiger that stopped growing. You can find cats behind grocery stores and under blankets. Cats can be confused with squirrels and raccoons; try not to make this serious mistake, as it will land you in the emergency room. You know you're talking to a cat if the animal has strings coming off its face and plays hard to get.

While cats have many great qualities, they struggle with pride. They're show-offs. They won't hesitate to rub it in your toddler's face that they are potty-trained. If your cat starts lowering your child's self-esteem, put on a video about lions to keep kitty's ego in check.

Things cats love: hugs, kisses on the nose, sudden movements, holding hands, sitting in boxes with you, being trapped, and more hugs. If you're chasing a cat, run fast and make a ruckus. Cats like to play hide-and-seek. Find them even if it takes all day. If a cat bites you with its hands or teeth, hold a grudge for at least twenty-four hours.

Enemies: Much like the cats on TV, cats in real life have enemies. Cat enemies include:

- Birds. Especially yellow ones.
- Smaller cats, stranger cats, and older cats. Think about it.
- Baths (cats dissolve in water).
- Spray bottles (see above).

Before getting a cat, make sure you have the proper supplies to make your kitty feel like part of the family.

- Brush or comb for your cat's hair. In a pinch, you can use a LEGO or a slice of bread (not a banana).
- Cat food. This comes in small cans and bags. People can eat it.
- A small bowl of water on the floor. Encourage your toddler to take sips; this is how your cat will develop a sense of community and be less selfish.
- A tray full of sand where cats go to the bathroom and your toddler has free play.
- Pieces of dust and hair for your cat to chase.

It's important to exercise your cat each and every day. Cats are known as the laziest animals on earth. If you let them, they'll sleep on large furniture or in closets all day. Don't allow this to happen. Your cat may resist stair drills and push-ups at first, but if you keep it up, your cat will learn to love physical fitness.

Now you're ready to find or buy a cat of your very own! Let your toddler name your cat and love it severely.

Dogs

You should definitely have four or five dogs in your home. Dogs are toddlers' closest animal relations. Toddlers love floor food; dogs love floor food. Toddlers love treats and rewards; so do dogs. Toddlers dream of being able to use the outside as a bathroom; dogs live this reality every day. Bring a dog into your home, and your child will have a best friend for life.

Dogs, much like horses, love giving free rides. Look for a small saddle.

Check: Does your dog have a tail? It will grow if you pull it just a little bit.

Dogs love to share their water and food. Help yourself. Just like toddlers, young dogs may have the occasional accident. As with your toddler, you shouldn't make a big deal.

Ironically, the number one enemy of dogs is cats. On television, you'll see a lot of dogs and cats being friendly, but that's only because they're getting paid. The number two enemy of dogs is rules.

Before getting a dog, make sure you have the following supplies:

- Shovel for poo
- Rug to absorb pee
- Food. Get the crunchy kind, that's my favorite.

Your toddler will not learn one thing about responsibility from owning a dog, but who cares.

Fish

Fish are quitters with weak spirits. They do not enjoy juice or hugs. If you feed a fish too much, it'll stop swimming with any kind of enthusiasm and go with the tide.

Ants

These are the only pets that we kill intentionally. Stomp away. Do your worst. They're spicy and best enjoyed with a piece of mild cheese. Ants are born in the wild but love to take up residence in homes where there is climate control. While they have a reputation for being disciplined workers, you'll never see an ant do an honest day's work. Instead, they appear to live off the crumbs of children. Someone once told me that ants are very strong. This must mean that I have the strength of Zeus, because I've defeated more than I can count.

Mice

I recently saw an episode of an old reality show called *Tom and Jerry*. The show features a sad domestic situation between a mouse who enjoys causing problems and his roommate, a mangy feline. What I learned is that, generally, mice enjoy instigating. Don't get into it with them.

Even if you don't go out and get a mouse, one may take a liking to you and move in uninvited. The proper thing to do is make a tiny bed for it out of a box of matches, like in books. It can bunk in the same room as your toddler and eat the same meals (only smaller). If your mouse starts dropping anvils on your head or trying to explode your personal belongings with dynamite, I told you so.

Snakes

You want to get your toddler a snake? Have you not seen the movie *Anaconda*? Where would you even get a snake? Do you have family friends in the rain forest? Do you regularly make bad choices, or is this an isolated incident? Speechless.

Owls

Owls are evil and haunted. They can taste with their eyes and do not like children. Every eight minutes, an owl captures another soul and places it in a BPA-free container. There are few people on earth who have seen an owl, and none of them is alive to tell the tale. If you sense an owl nearby, look for an opening in a nearby tree. Crawl into it and hide. Call a friend. When he arrives, distract your buddy with a leaf and then suddenly jump out of the tree and run for your life. The owl will pursue your friend while you flee to safety.

Horses

If you're lucky enough to have a horse, consider adopting me. You'll be interested to know that I don't currently have any savings. Every time my grandpa gives me twenty dollars, my mother snatches it the minute he leaves the house. I believe she uses it to stay knee-deep in Baked! Lay's. If you look out your back window and see horses, please add me to your checking account and send a debit card that I can use at my leisure. Don't include the PIN in the same envelope, as we must think of our family's financial security. I look forward to being your best friend and newest dependent.

Infants

Though young babies are in demand, I do not recommend picking one up. Like a bacterial infection, it will quickly take over your home and become the center of attention. The problem with infants is that they don't care who was there before them. If someone brings a small baby into your home, do your best to keep it quiet with milk and blankets, then pack your things and move out during the night. If you choose to stay, say goodbye to your lifestyle. Pet babies are more work than you can imagine, and will almost never pay off. Do not expect your pet infant to ever compliment you. It will talk behind your back and ruin your career. If your friends are getting these, don't feel pressured. Just sit back and laugh when it all blows up in their faces.

Rocks

Smart toddlers love collecting pebbles and caring for them. Your problem with this makes me think you're jealous. You're jealous of a rock.

Choose your rock carefully. It should have a pleasant disposition and be mature enough to leave its family of origin. Landscaped yards often have a beautiful selection. Go ahead and steal (borrow for life). Wash your rock in your mouth at least once a week. This has less to do with cleanliness and more to do with maintaining intimacy. For the first eight weeks, cosleep with your rock until it becomes acclimated to your environment. Feed your rock a steady diet of . . . LOVE! They also like ice-cream sandwiches, but keep these a sometime food.

Before you do a load of laundry, check your toddler's pockets for pet rocks. It's crazy that I have to say this, but do not throw your toddler's friend and confidant in the garbage. Though you may not understand the bond, that is no reason to disrespect or destroy it.

Pop Quiz

1. If I already have a cat, and a mouse moves into my home, the first thing I should do is:
   a. Start filming.
   b. Get a dog to balance things out.
   c. (a) and (b)

2. I have a horse. Should I reach out to a toddler who may need more belongings?
   a. Yes.
   b. Yes.

3. An owl asks to be your valentine. You:
   a. Get excited and immediately change your Facebook relationship status.
   b. Lure it into a burlap sack with chocolates and sell it to a passerby.
   c. Buy it flowers.

4. True or false: In a pinch, fish can replace ninja stars.
   a. True.
   b. False.

5. Why do dogs lick water instead of bringing the bowl to their lips?
   a. No working fingers.
   b. To make it last longer.
   c. They're trying to be cute.
   d. Fear of failure.
   e. All of the above.

6. Answer Key: 1: c 2: a 3: b 4: a 5: e

- -

Homework: Keep taking the above quiz until you don't get an F.

- -

The number one thing to remember about animals is that they need love. Most of them want to be held tight but are too afraid to ask. Just do it until they relax.

Note: Your child may, from time to time, shape shift into a dog or other animal. Toddlers are method actors and will take their commitments to these roles very far. Poo on the carpet far. Just go with it.

TODDLER'S CORNER

Dear HT,

Sometimes when I do something, my mom or dad leans in too close and says, "WE don't do that." What do they mean?

—Independent Woman, twenty-six months old, New Jersey

Dear Independent,

First off, you're two. No need to calculate your age in months just because your mom does. She's crazy.

Ah yes, the royal "we." Parents and caregivers use this word to convince you that you are incapable of original ideas. Toddlers around the world hear it on a regular basis.

- *We look with our eyes.*
- *We don't hit.*
- *We stay out of the trash can.*

No, Mommy, YOU look with your eyes. YOU don't hit. YOU stay out of the trash can. I DO ALL OF THE ABOVE AND MORE. How do they know who we are? They don't. But they're intent on telling us. The next time you hear "We don't____," just stare blankly with your mouth slightly open, like a red snapper, and wait for an opportunity to carry on with your important business.

We. What, are we in a gang? Are you the human resources of my life? Is this the Scouts?

Are you a colonist? No. Please, old people, keep your generational limitations to yourself, and allow toddlers to forge their own way. Stop projecting your weaknesses.

Take a lesson from Dora. Does she say "Swiper, no swipin' " or "Hey, Swiper, how ya doing? Okay, look, WE don't swipe."

Toddlers should start throwing out their own "we."

- Mommy, WE don't buy clothes that don't currently fit.
- Daddy, WE don't act like we don't know how to load the dishwasher to get out of doing dishes.
- Mommy, WE don't fall asleep on the living room floor while playing LEGOs.
- Daddy, WE don't pretend that WE can't smell my chocolate-thunder diaper explosions.

See? It can go both ways. Save the passive-aggressive conformist syntax for another baby, because we're done.

Do you, Independent. Do you.

xo, HT

11

More Tips
for Effective and Brief Communication
with Your Toddler

Life isn't easy for a toddler. One minute your parents are champing at the bit for you to speak; a few months later, they're looking at you with faraway eyes, barely listening. Every word that comes out of your toddler's mouth needs to be hungrily consumed like golden nectar straight from heaven. Verbal ambrosia, if you will. Whether it be a string of vowels or a twenty-minute story about birds, soak it up. You'll never hear anything better.

"No"

While the word "no" has only one meaning in the more primitive forms of English such as the dialect that adults speak, the toddler "no" is rich with interpretations. Did you know that there are more than four hundred different meanings for "no" in Toddler English? Most of them are none of your business, but I've included an abbreviated list.

What We Say	What We Mean
NO.	NO.
NO.	I'm too angry/tired to think.
NO.	I'm not sure.
NO.	Please repeat the question.
NO.	Who are you?
NO.	I need to be alone right now.
NO.	Yes.
NO.	You have exhausted me in both body and mind.
NO.	I am three seconds from striking you.
NO.	Stop talking to me.
NO.	I am coming unhinged.

The quicker you learn to distinguish between these NOs, the better life will be. It might help to carry around a notepad and recording device for the purpose of studying on your own time.

Toddler Monologues

Some people think a normal conversation includes ideas from both parties. This is not accurate. When your toddler is sharing a story with you, whether it's about squirrels or a friend who does not currently exist, do not mistake a breathing pause or rhetorical question as a cue for you to speak.

From Wikipedia: *In theatre, a monologue (or monolog) is a speech presented by a single character, most often to express his thoughts aloud, though sometimes also to directly address another character or the audience.*

A conversation with the special 2T in your life will most likely require you to put on your listening ears and keep your talking mouth silent. Don't be upset. Not everything can be about you. If your toddler is ahead of her time, you may notice factual discrepancies within her amazing tale that you will classify incorrectly as lies. Again, you are overstepping and jumping to conclusions; your task is to listen without judgment.

Toddler stories usually feature a very important transition statement: "and then." When you hear "and then," hold on to your hat, because a plot twist is right around the corner, and it will blow all of your assumptions about life out the window. Keep in mind that "and then" does not necessarily mean that something takes place after something. It can also mean "before" and "never."

If the toddler you are conversing with is a stranger, you can still learn something new by giving your full attention to his narrative. Even if it means not getting off at the bus stop you'd intended, or being unable to board your flight, it's important to show the same respect to the strange child that you would your own and let the fable run its course.

How long will your toddler's commentary last? Why, do you have somewhere to be? Is supporting the fruit of your loins' creativity getting in the way of your very important schedule? Is the queen of England waiting on you for afternoon sandwiches? Are you cohosting the Grammys? Is a summit on science where you are the key presenter being delayed because you're the only one who knows how to turn on the slide projector? Are you scheduled to orbit into space within the hour? Are you a veterinarian, and is there a lion at the zoo waiting for you to perform emergency tail surgery? Are you late for an appointment with the person who invented fire? Are you currently peeing your pants and can't deal with a little moisture? Please explain why you're in such a rush. That's what I thought. Now sit down.

Dos and Don'ts When Enjoying a Toddler Story

- **DON'T** question the author's authority on the topic or facts. If water flies into a rainbow and shatters into poo flakes, then water flies into a rainbow and shatters into poo flakes. It's called poetry. Heard of it?

- **DO** nod and smile. The look on your face should be a cross between "You are so beautiful" and "This is the best thing I've ever heard thank you please keep on going forever."
- **DON'T** look at the clock unless you're competing in a rudeness competition sponsored by Guinness World Records.
- **DO** invite others to come hear the story with a quick motion of your hand.
- **DON'T** fall asleep. You will be awakened with a swift slap to the face.
- **DO** mouth the word "wow" several times.
- **DON'T** break eye contact with your toddler.
- **DO** make your eyes bright and eager like a young fox's.
- **DON'T** stand up and slowly back away.
- **DO** periodically hand your child gummy bears to keep her stamina at optimal levels.

If you find yourself unteachable, take up an apprenticeship with a grandma in your area. Watch how she encourages a lap seat and puts both arms around her sweet baby. Grandma's face will never be more than seven to eight inches from her toddler's as she soaks up every moment of the experience. Her expression will clearly say, "This is the most entertaining speech I've had the privilege of listening to," and she means it. When the tale wraps up, you'll notice that Grandma already has a SNACK PREPARED to reward her little word maestro. No, this will not be expired rice cakes on a paper towel. We're talking about baked goods made with love and effort earlier that day. If you don't know what baked goods look like, just use Google. Search "baked goods cake fresh."

Help

Toddlers are a very proud species. Asking for help is difficult. One of the many reasons why it is essential to hover over your child is to protect him from the humiliation of having to make a verbal request for assistance. If, for some reason, you get caught up in Facebook and don't spot trouble before it arrives, your child may ask for help in a variety of untraditional ways to save face.

1. **Breaking items:** A particularly angry toddler may choose to stomp a toy unrecognizable. Rush over. No judgment, please. Just replace it and forgive yourself.
2. **Inconsolable tears:** You've really dropped the ball, haven't you? When a young and gifted child needs help putting on her socks, it's important that you show up before her shirt is soaked in a sea of sadness.
3. **Clothing removal:** We've touched on the many reasons why your toddler might feel the need to go nude. A cry for help is one of them.
4. **Slapping:** Handle this gracefully and without punishment. I know what you're thinking: "Why didn't my toddler just calmly ask for help in a form of English I'm more familiar with?" Most likely, your child *did* ask for help in her mind several times before resorting to unconventional methods of communication. Seems like those parenting instincts you speak of so much aren't as strong as you'd like to believe.

Screaming

Toddlers don't scream for no reason at all. Science has proved that twenty to thirty daily screams help your toddler's lungs grow into maturity. The next time your child's battle cry makes you lose hearing/vision for a few minutes, say, "Thanks, science!" instead of closing your eyes.

There are several varieties of the toddler scream. The better you get to know them, the faster they'll become your friends.

Recreational Scream

This yell accompanies twinkling laughter and is best described as an overflow of pure delight. You won't be expecting it, so your blood may run cold. If your heart stops, just pound your chest. If you look around, you'll notice that nothing is wrong and your toddler is just having the time of his life.

Rage Scream

Disobedient toys. Water that can't listen. The reasons your toddler might roar in anger are endless. This scream needs to be treated with respect or it will be quickly followed with Berserk. Berserk is when your toddler does windmill arms and tries to break everything in sight, including your face.

Cry Scream

Sometimes, when a toddler is crying, tears just aren't enough. She'll take a deep breath and let out a vocal lamentation that will definitely turn heads if you happen to be in public. If there are any dogs around, they will instinctively begin to howl in unison.

Fun Facts on Toddler Communication

- Just because a toddler is looking at you and speaking doesn't mean she's talking to you.
- Just because a toddler makes direct eye contact and says your name doesn't mean she's talking to you.
- At any given time, there are six or seven imaginary friends with whom your toddler may be in deep conversation. Don't interrupt. You don't know these people.
- Toddlers often begin stories in the middle, return to the begin-

ning, and then end with a dramatic finale. You can easily keep up if you try.

Some parents think it's their job to make a toddler communicate in the same way they do. I'm shaking my head, but you can't see me. You are a caregiver, not a colonizer. You are a visitor in the land of toddlertopia. After your passport has been stamped, it's your responsibility to assimilate.

Note on Loud Noises: Toddler Kryptonite

Ninety-nine percent of toddlers are personally offended by loud noises. These include but are not limited to: cars backfiring, airplanes landing, and blenders making soup that nobody asked for. If you want your toddler to become a stable adult who can pass a credit check, you must protect his delicate sensibilities now. The guide below will show you how to operate household appliances and lead your toddler through a medium-noise-level life.

Blenders

Toddlers love smoothies, but the grating, crushing sound of blenders upsets their homeostasis. You may not know this, but you can purchase smoothies outside the home for a small fee. If you have your heart set on making one at home, do so. The most common recipe calls for three parts ice cream to one part juice. Before you turn on your blender, throw a large blanket over the device to muffle the noise. Opt for a thick comforter. Go under the blanket tent to turn your blender on and off. Your toddler thanks you for your consideration.

Vacuum Cleaners

I'm not sure when regular brooms went out of style, but these days every parent wants to own a vacuum cleaner. These robots will stop at nothing to terrorize the children and small animals in your home by chasing them and eating their small toys/snacks, all while making sounds reminiscent of a localized tornado. The best solution to vacuum noise is not to allow one into your home. No amount of Chex debris is worth your toddler having an emotional breakdown.

Outside Sounds

Motorcycles, fire engines . . . the list goes on and on, and while you can't always prevent the sounds that float into your toddler's ears from the street, you can stop them once they start. Did you know that if a mother grizzly bear senses a threat within a six-mile proximity of her cub, she will immediately eliminate it? Bears don't ask questions, and neither should you. If a recycling truck makes your toddler jump out of his pants, stand in your doorway and throw a rock through the truck's front window. If someone is using a leaf blower and your toddler can't hear her TV shows, run outside, grab the device, and break it over your leg. By taking appropriate action, you are telling the world to watch its back, because when it comes to your sweet angel, you are unstoppable.

Other Children

The sounds of stranger children enjoying themselves can be upsetting. Shrieks and yells of happiness are a welcome noise when your toddler is a part of the action, but from the sidelines, they sound like butternut squash tastes (terrible). If the children at your neighborhood park or in the yard adjacent to yours are living it up in a way that angers your child, find a way to sabotage the activities. If you have a hose, spray them. Not in a fun "it's summertime" way but in a more aggressive fashion, making it clear that you're trying to cleanse them of joy. Aim above the neck.

More Tips

Homework: (1) Go one full day without speaking. Love it so much that you make it a regular thing. (2) If your toddler's voice gets hoarse from yelling, offer a cough drop. Sugar cubes are the same as cough drops. If you're all out of cubes, loose grain sugar can also soothe a young esophagus.

Dear Honest Toddler,

I would love to experience a calm car trip with my three-year-old. Please send your advice.
Love, Getting a migraine in Laguna Beach, CA

Dear Migraine,

At this time alternate reality technology is not available to the general public but I've heard you can go anywhere in your imagination.

Thanks, HT

12

Car Etiquette
(and Places to Avoid Visiting)

So you say you need to drive somewhere. I only partially believe you. Your lies aside, it's important to prepare your toddler for every vehicular excursion.

Snacks

Here's a comprehensive list of the snacks you need to have in your car at all times.

- 2 snack packs of crackers
- 3 to 4 string cheeses
- 1 small Ziploc bag of raisins
- 12 ounces of sliced turkey breast
- 2 full-sized peanut-butter-and-jelly sandwiches cut into eighths
- 8 jumbo marshmallows
- Baker's dozen of assorted old-fashioned doughnuts
- 10 juice boxes (apple)
- Medium-sized jar of rainwater
- 1 box of cereal
- 1 handful of baking powder (to simulate snow in emergencies)

- 2 pounds of saltwater taffy
- 1 toasted and buttered English muffin
- 1 bag of Hershey's Kisses (for bribes)

Once you've stocked up on the essentials, beckon your toddler in a gentle voice to join you on a journey.

The Trip

Explain to your toddler that you will be going on a short ride to the ice-cream store. You're thinking, "But we're not going to the ice-cream store." Yes, you are. You actually are.

Find an appropriate car seat. It WILL NOT feature one of the popular five-point-harness restraints that induce rage in so many children. Find a car seat that allows for 100 percent mobility throughout the vehicle. Your toddler should be able to climb easily from the trunk area to under the steering wheel with few restrictions. If you can't find one of these car seats in stores, you can modify the one you already have by cutting off all of the straps.

Once you've started the car and your toddler has removed his shoes, throw the snacks in the air to create a confetti potluck. You'll notice a strange look on your toddler's face. This is called happiness. You probably haven't seen it before. Keep your wits about you. Once you're on the road, your toddler will make a variety of requests. Many of them will be unclear. Meet them all. Be sure to point out interesting things to see, such as planes, construction sites, dogs, and mailboxes. Don't miss any.

DO NOT leave your toddler in the car to "just run in" a store. What's wrong with you?

Make this trip a short one; eight to nine minutes from start to finish is ideal. Five to six minutes should be spent pulled over with your toddler in your lap, playing with the steering wheel and radio dials. Once you've arrived back at home, give your toddler the following questionnaire for customer-service evaluation.

Car Etiquette

Motor-Vehicle Excursion Performance Summary

1. I felt this trip was justified .... yes/no
2. My emotional needs were met during this trip .... yes/no
3. A toy was purchased for me on this trip............................. yes/no
4. A snack was purchased for me on this trip .... yes/no
5. We went somewhere fun and amazing .... yes/no
6. I would take another trip with this driver.......................... yes/no
7. When we arrived at home, I was immediately removed
   from the car and the adult in question did not linger ...... yes/no

1—Always   2—Sometimes   3—Never

8. The person driving took my requests seriously._____
9. The person driving did not let the freeway get between him/her
   and the hugs I needed._____
10. The person behind the wheel cares about me._____
11. This driver enjoys the company of small children.
    _____
12. When I asked for food, it was handed back in a timely fashion and
    did not require too much arm reaching on my part._____

Use this form as a motivational tool. If you reach for the stars today and every day, you will notice a dramatic improvement in your abilities.

Note: If you pick up strangers from the airport, they should never be seated next to your toddler. Either the front seat, next to you, or nothing. This is why taxis were invented.

Car Music

By toddlerhood, your child will already have a favorite song. This tune will be playing constantly in your little one's head, especially while you are rambling. During car trips, it is important that you put your toddler's jam on repeat. Though variety may be the spice of life, we all know that spices are constantly ruining perfectly good meals. Consistency is the frosting of life. In the case of savory foods, consistency is the ketchup of life. Do you see where I'm going with this?

If your toddler's special song isn't your favorite, invest in a Discman and a pair of headphones for trips; you can listen to whatever you want. Just be sure to put one side of the headphones on your temple, like a DJ, so you can hear your child's requests clearly. That's pretty much common sense, but I know by now to spell it out.

Traffic

When a car slows to barely moving for several minutes, many toddlers come unhinged. The hysterical screaming you're hearing from the backseat isn't theatrics or negative behavior that you can cure with half-truths, like "We'll be there soon." You need to make it go away. For once, concentrate. Focus your mind on moving the cars in front of you. Visualize the vehicles in your path rolling away, making a clearing for you to drive at eighty-plus miles an hour. Toddlers take traffic very personally, and if an unbroken sense of faith in the world means anything to you, you'll do everything in your power to prevent it.

For inspiration to cultivate your special abilities, watch shows with heroes like Superman and Professor Xavier from *X-Men*. You'll notice that despite the wonderfulness of these people, they stayed humble and did not try to control those around them. How did that truth affect your heart?

If your brain waves won't budge, keep at least four wrapped gifts in your glove compartment for emergencies. The presents should have a retail value of at least twenty dollars each, so no dollar-store goodies, have I made myself clear?

If you lack both money and superpowers, I'm surprised you've come this far in life. You have no choice other than to entertain your toddler by ramming other vehicles. When you're in jail, rest assured that your toddler probably will visit you every now and again, depending.

Cleanliness

Car commercials will try to convince you that the inside of your motor vehicle should be spotless and free of soiled diapers. That's not true. As long as you use the sticky tabs on the diaper to form it into a tight sphere, it can be part of the natural car habitat. The reason that so many car interiors are made of fabric is so they can absorb juice, pee-pee, the occasional surprise vomit, and blood. These liquids get pulled by gravity through the seat's surface and will dry overnight. You could say that cars are self-cleaning.

Gas-station vacuums are loud and terrifying devices. Their long trunks want to hurt your baby. Just don't worry your head about the beach of Cheerio and Goldfish cracker crumbs on the interior floor, because it's trail mix to a hungry child. Trust me, your toddler will enjoy the snack at a later date.

To make you feel better about your vehicle, I took a visual inventory and have included a list of all the exciting items I spotted within my family's car.

16 Cheez-Its

1 box of Band-Aids (empty—all used justifiably)

2 empty juice boxes

42 receipts

9 individual toddler-sized dirty socks

1 clean sock

A change of emergency clothes, one size too small

1 hard-boiled egg in shell

3 individual bootleg Crocs, 1 real

$2.30 in change

1 clump of hair

5 bank brochures on home mortgages, stolen by yours truly

Fine layer of borrowed park sand
5 diapers in three sizes

This was all within a one-foot radius. We don't worry about it, and neither should you.

Pop Quiz: Dealing with Common Car Problems

If you're in a car with a toddler, there's a 100 percent chance that an issue will arise. You may recognize some of the scenarios below. Test your knowledge of toddlers and your ability to parent by completing the following quiz.

Situation #1

You're driving ninety miles an hour, and your toddler needs help peeling a clementine. She is very hungry. Do you:

a. Locate the nearest exit in a timely fashion. Pull over and proceed to peel the clementine.
b. Keep driving and hope that your toddler can metabolize her feelings of disappointment.
c. Reach back while not taking your eyes off the road and peel the clementine with one hand, being sure not to pierce the fruit's delicate skin.

If you chose (a), then the joke's on you, because your child will have already blacked out from hunger by the time you find an exit. Way to take your time.

If you chose (b), then I'm not quite sure why you chose parenthood. It's possible you had a passion for serving others at one point, but it's gone now.

If you chose (c), then give yourself a gold star! If you have only one gold star, give it to your toddler and help yourself to a shipping label.

Situation #2

Your best friend needs a ride. She wants to listen to the news, but your toddler needs to hear her favorite song. Do you:

a. Explain to your toddler that sometimes we have to take turns and turn the dial to NPR.
b. Distract your friend by asking what her favorite color is and then push her out of the moving vehicle.
c. Not give your friend a ride in the first place, because what does that have to do with your toddler, and she's a stranger.

If you chose (a), then I need to know if you've ever heard the phrase "blood is thicker than water." The saying has nothing to do with cooking and everything to do with choices. FAMILY FIRST EVERY TIME.

If you chose (b), then you have earned my respect. That is hilarious.

If you chose (c), then you were born for this job. Bravo.

Situation #3

Your toddler finds her car seat uncomfortable and refuses to sit down or relax from plank position. Do you:

a. Yell threats in the voice of the warden from *The Shawshank Redemption* and try to break your toddler's stiff body in half with forceful pushing.
b. Collapse into dramatic tears from stress. Give up and sit in the parked car with your eyes closed while your child plays in the back.
c. Abandon your plans for the day.

If you chose (a), then please call your nearest police department and turn yourself in. Wow.

If you chose (b), then you're on the right track. This could get even better if there were snacks involved. I like your thought process and see your potential. B+.

If you chose (c), then I think you should be an ambassador. Someone with your level of integrity deserves an official title, sash, and a few pins. Enjoy being the best.

Situation #4

Your toddler has removed one shoe and thrown it out the window. Do you:

   a. Stop buying shoes, after realizing what a waste of funds they are, and make a Certificate of Good Thinking for your toddler using your home computer.
   b. Park the car and search for the shoe while muttering angrily to yourself like a crazy person.
   c. Answer (b), plus tell the other parent, Santa, and/or Facebook.

If you chose (a), then please consider applying for my godmother or godfather position. It is currently filled, but I can see to it that a space opens up.

If you chose (b), then I'm not that mad, because your toddler is probably getting a good laugh. Park in a way that allows your child to watch while you search (for entertainment purposes).

If you chose (c), then you sound like you need some time to yourself and possibly a nap, but since you have a child, that is out of the question. Pull yourself together for the sake of your family. No tattling.

(Print Out) Apology Note to Other Drivers

You are legally impaired when driving with a toddler. Below is a note you can distribute to other motorists or the police if you are pulled over.

Dear Ma'am or Sir or Law-Enforcement Officer,

I just want to start off with an apology. The reason I [circle one: swerved, am driving so slow, changed lanes unpredictably, cut you off] is because my toddler had a legitimate emergency. He/she had to [circle one: use the bathroom, remove himself/herself from the car seat, have something handed back], and I'm not the type of parent to ignore a cry for help.

I don't deserve this ticket/verbal assault.

I am a great driver, but being a parent means putting your needs fourth or fifth. Perhaps if there were people standing on the side of the road handing out juice boxes and assorted toys, like they do for marathon runners, traveling by car would be easier for my sweet baby. It is very difficult for a small, muscular child to be confined for extended periods of time, so I know you understand why I made the choices I did.

If you are a police-person standing next to my car, please do not judge the interior. It does not smell like [circle one: old food, urine] in here; that is just your active imagination. If you are deciding whether or not to give me a moving violation, it's good for you to know that it will be paid with my child's college fund. I'm sure you don't want another person on the streets, so make your choice wisely.

Love, _____ [your name]

Where NOT to Go: Avoiding Toddler Danger Zones

Unfortunately, there are places you can go that are hostile environments for a sensitive young child such as yours. Learn and then delete these locations from your GPS.

Churches/Synagogues/Mosques/Any Places of Worship

Children under four have only one volume level: disruptive. Our vocal cords are not capable of whispering. While toddlers respect all faiths, being asked to keep low tones for fear of persecution violates our personal freedom. Believe anything you like, but it is unreasonable to expect your toddler to sit through a ceremony in which neither gifts nor fries will be distributed.

If you're considering bringing your toddler to your special building, do so with a relaxed attitude. Repeat after me: "I don't care what anyone thinks of my family, my parenting, or my child. They can all kick rocks." Allowing yourself to worry about strangers giving you side-eye as your toddler crawls under pews or makes small rips in sacred texts will cause stress in your already rapidly aging body. Reframe your experience: Is your toddler kicking the back of pews or spiritually downloading a sick beat from above? Who's to know?

Some places of worship have child care. I can confidently say that these are not safe places. Drop by to pick up a to-go box of their snacks, but don't hang around, and DO NOT leave your toddler with these hippies. Most religions believe that you should treat people how you want to be treated. Would you like to be left at doggy day care?

- -

Homework: Pray at home.

- -

Libraries

Don't even bother. The last time I went to one of these places, everyone was whispering, as if books could hear. Thankfully, I'm not a fool, so I talked at top volume. A library is like a bookstore for the broke. You go there to openly steal. While this sounds like a good time, the 947 rules put a damper on the possibility of a positive experience. People who work and seemingly live at the library do not want you to be yourself. Running up and down stairs will earn you a one-way ticket out the back door.

Story time isn't much better. Imagine sitting in a circle with acquaintances, chanting spells and being drilled on a variety of subjects. "What sound does a duck make?" Who cares? When will I need to know that? How is this knowledge of barnyard animals and their corresponding noises going to improve my life? Toddlers who get up to stretch their legs or explore will be publicly admonished. The participation reward will not be a glazed doughnut, so don't bother.

Homework: Visit your local library and cause a scene. Notice how great you feel.

Banks

Banks are terrible places, with a variety of brochures fresh for the taking. Your toddler will probably grab close to twenty. It's fine. Toddlers have a very difficult time at the bank, because there isn't much to see other than the legs of adults. It's like a forest of pants. If you say things like "Stand still," you're missing the whole point of childhood. And yes, those seat-belt-material line dividers are for playing with, so just relax.

Post Offices

Have a letter to send? Invest in a Harry Potter–style messenger owl, or forget the whole thing. The post office plays with your toddler's heart by displaying a bounty of unavailable paper goods. If your child were to, say, open a box of return envelopes, hide them under the stroller. Please visit the post office alone once your toddler is an adult. You don't need to apply for a passport, as you aren't going anywhere.

Homework: Buy a new car. Search for one without doors so your toddler can come and go as she pleases. Draw a map of all the play centers and candy factories in your area, and make it a priority to visit each of them this week. Avoid most other places. It'll feel great to do something for others.

Dear Honest Toddler,

Do you know where I can find toddler-sized '80s rock band concert tees? I'm trying to look worldly.

Sincerely, Trying Hard in West Virginia

Dear Trying,

Your toddler is not a living memorial to your interests. You're embarrassing yourself.

Love, HT

13

Breakdown of Popular Toddler Trends, from Amber Necklaces to Jeggings, and Why You Should Avoid Them

Everywhere you look, you'll find books, clothes, and devices promising a happier, more prosperous life with your toddler. One of the many hats I wear is that of consumer advocate. Heed my advice if you wish to protect yourself from the myriad snake-oil salesmen on the prowl for gullible parents.

Amber Necklaces

Parents struggle with teething. I mean, toddlers are the ones physically suffering what feels like flaming-hot Tic Tacs cutting through their gums, but from the way parents speak, you'd think they were the ones in pain. A few years ago, someone somewhere decided that sap, the actual poo-poo from trees, could heal children from teething discomfort and fevers. Since then, parents have been throwing money at Etsy, trying to get their hands on one of these magic necklaces. I'm wearing one right now. Not one adult asked, "What does science have to say about this?" I commissioned a lab in England to run tests on these amber necklaces, and the results were shocking. No, they do not help relieve the discomfort from teething, but they do increase whining by 45 percent.

Jeggings

While stretch material is ideal for the toddler body type, when you stuff your child's thighs into denim-printed Lycra-spandex blends, you make a mockery of her. No toddler needs to walk around in pants that appear to have been painted on. So many of us have not made the transition to the potty. When jeggings are paired with a diaper, the end result is a derriere three times its normal size. Unless you think it's cute for young children to dress as if they're "dropping it like it's hot" at the club, stick to normal pants.

Leashes

Everybody knows a runner: the kind of toddler who waits like a jaguar in the savannah for the perfect opportunity to spring out of the bush and take off. I'm going to tell you right now that there is NOTHING more exhilarating than hearing an adult you love pursue you. The footsteps pounding behind you as your heart races, the frantic calls becoming shrieks. The final moment before they grab you by the midsection and swoop you into their arms. Everyone should experience it at least once.

In response to this toddler pastime, the good people at Master Lock have developed the toddler leash. Basically, it's a harness attached to crude rope. Recently, companies have dressed it up, making a backpack/stuffed animal attached to a "tail" that the adult holds. Either way, the child is being treated like a dog. I shape-shift into a Doberman on a regular basis, so I don't have a problem with toddler leashes as long as I'm not attached to one. I would love for more toddlers who aren't me to be put on leashes at the park. Especially the toddlers who think the swings are personal property and monopolize them to the point where other toddlers have to wait for hours. You know who I'm talking about, Charles. If you want to swing all day, put a swing set in your backyard. Everyone hates you for this. Ten-minute maximum.

Crocs

Everyone except parents knows that toddlers don't need shoes. Thankfully, a company called Crocs has invented a foot cover that fulfills most shoe requirements while maintaining a barely-there presence on your toddler's foot.

Why Toddlers Love Crocs
- They're easy to kick off.
- No need to destroy them; they're already full of holes.
- They look like cartoons.

Crocs can be dressed up for church weddings or meetings with the government. If you're low on funds, most dollar stores carry bootleg versions that will take you far in life. Walking around in Crocs tells the world that you care a little, but not too much.

Weird Strollers

There are a variety of strollers on the market—four, to be exact. Remember, at the end of the day, what matters is that your toddler doesn't have to walk. The ability to orbit into space or travel into other dimensions is not necessary, so please avoid strollers that look like they were commissioned by NASA. Parents, I know you want to turn heads, but again, this has nothing to do with you. Make sure the stroller isn't too heavy, as most of the time you'll be holding your child in your arms while pushing it.

Toddler Perfume

Let me start by saying that you don't always smell like roses yourself. Trying to mask the pungent odors that occasionally make their way out of your toddler's various orifices is futile. You may be able to Febreze car interiors, but your toddler is a poo-poo factory first and foremost. If you want to be surrounded by great smells, try baking something.

Discipline

I already know what you're thinking. "Is discipline a trend?" In a word, yes. There was a time when toddlers were free to run like banshees without a looming fear of naughty spots. The year was 1972, and juice ran through the streets like water. Now you can't push a baby down without having to take a time-out on the park bench like a criminal. What we need is rehabilitation, not time-outs. Stop counting to three. Nobody's scared. What are you going to do after you get to three? Freeze time? Rain down wrath in the form of hail and locusts? Silly.

If you knew how you look when you're enforcing rules, you'd stop. Your face takes on a werewolf-esque snarl. And you actually smell different (like trash in the summer). I wrote this poem as a gift to my mother after a particularly difficult week. Enjoy. Think about how you can apply it to your own life and reduce the amount of angry eyes and wrinkled foreheads in your home.

You Look Prettier When You Smile

Thanks for coming in last night
It's nice to know someone cares
My blanket was twisted
And I thought I heard bears

Breakdown of Popular Toddler Trends

You whispered promises and threats
For, LOL, quite a while
But next time remember
You look prettier when you smile

There's no need for scowls
When I want midnight water
Dehydration's a thing
Weren't you once a young daughter?

Please bring the right cup
I could drain the whole Nile
Relax your face, Mama
You look prettier when you smile

What's that in the hall?
It smells bad and looks fudgy
Was it caused by a child so beautiful and pudgy?
Why name names? Let's move on.

The poop's deep in the tile
Grab the Lysol, but keep in mind
You look prettier when you smile

I was dressed head to toe
Despite putting up a fight
We wrestled with pants
It took all of your might

Now my clothes can be found
In a haphazard pile
Are you mad? Hey, Mom:
You look prettier when you smile

You are my angel, day in and day out
But angels don't swear, and they definitely don't shout
So when we're together and I do something vile
Keep the crazy eyes in check
You look prettier when you smile

Preschools

First, toddlers don't need no school. Once a child has reached the toddler stage, he pretty much knows what life is about. If you're spending hundreds or even thousands of dollars every month so that your kid can stuff Play-Doh up his nose, you should have just flushed that money down the toilet; at least then you would have had something cool to watch. Don't believe me? Flush something. Anything. If it's smaller than an orange, it'll go down. If it's bigger, you'll create a tidal wave. Win/win.

Socialization is not a real reason to enroll your child in school. Toddlers will learn to pretend they like people on their own time. Take the money you would have wasted on school and put it toward something useful, like a bounce house.

If you are still tempted to sign your child up for school, be aware that most toddlers will make the experience as painful for you as it is for us. Popular methods of parental punishment include:

1. **Calling the teacher Mommy** (male or female, doesn't matter).
2. **Revealing secrets from home.** Yes, your child's teacher will know that Daddy has been sleeping on the sofa bed for the past few nights and that Mommy bleaches her mustache.
3. **Biting other children.** Nothing says "I have no home training" like drawing blood from a friend with your mouth.
4. **Streaking.**

I was recently sent a heart-wrenching letter from a two-and-a-half-year-old recounting her first day of preschool. Grab a tissue.

Hi HT,

My small night-light is my only source of illumination as I write this. It's ironic, really—not only have the lights in my home gone out for the evening; earlier today they went out in my soul. From my crib, I can hear them watching their prime-time shows, greedily plunging their hands into my cereal . . . I've been left alone to process this dark day's events while they enjoy an evening of leisure.

When I arose from deep slumber, damp with urine that had leaked through my drugstore-brand diapers, I eagerly anticipated a morning rich with the melodic genius of the Backyardigans. Instead, my body was pushed and shoved into clean clothes and new shoes. Surely we were going to the fair, I surmised. Mother was nervous. Father seemed giddy. As I watched the trees whiz past our car, a naive smile played across my lips. I thought of the cotton candy, the merry-go-round, and the hot dogs that I believed were in my very near future.

Then we pulled up to a building I'd never seen. Inside, the sounds of young voices and the smell of children in various states of cleanliness overwhelmed me. Instinctively, I grabbed for Mother and demanded up. She held me close; it seemed she was as scared as I was. I whispered "Let us flee this place" in her ear, but it came out as "NOOOOOOOOOOOOOOOOOOOOOOOOOO!" Before I could process what was happening, I was in a brightly colored room. What was all this construction paper compensating for? What institution hides under such a thin guise of whimsy? My head was spinning. To my left, a little girl was stacking blocks. To my right, a boy not over three was having a loud response and had begun removing his clothes.

I turned and noticed Mother's and Father's faces close to mine as they crouched down to my level. I couldn't hear what they said over the screams in my head, but I'm sure it was "Goodbye forever." They hugged me, kissed me, and while I'm still in denial that this is even possible, they left.

I cried. Oh, how I cried.

Then we played. It was terrible. Terribly fun, but that doesn't change anything.

Fourteen hours later, Father returned as if nothing had happened. We packed up my belongings and left. Where we go from here, I don't know. While part of me craves the almost otherwordly snack-time delicacies I experienced this afternoon—cream cheese on a graham cracker, heaven—my world has been shaken.

Share my story, HT. And take heed. This could happen to you.

Sincerely, Amy (two-and-a-half years old)

I've never read anything so sad. If anyone knows where I can get some of those crackers with cream cheese, let me know.

- -

Homework: File a preemptive restraining order against the preschools in your area.

- -

· · ·

To: Mommy

From: Sweet Baby aka Angel Face aka a helpless child

Subject: Last night . . .

Hi. I just have a quick question—I know we have a busy day ahead, of me watching you do things—but what does love mean to you? I'm curious.

To me, it means rising from bed with a sense of urgency when your darling needs something to drink at midnight, two A.M., and finally, four-forty-five without making a big deal. I can't see your scowl in the dark, but I can hear your dramatic sigh, and frankly, it's a little off-putting.

Customer service isn't just about providing what's been asked for; it's about attitude and delivery. As your supervisor, I find your "I'd rather be anywhere but here" air of insolence not only damaging to our relationship but a threat to the fragile foundation of trust in others that I'm struggling to develop.

You tell me that you love me all the time, but maybe you should start saying "I love you when I'm fully rested," because whispering things like "This is the last time I'm coming in here" directly contradicts your daytime sentiments. When a demon touches my face in the dead of night, causing me to cry out, I need you to run, not walk, to my side.

Do people who love each other lie to each other? If not, where's the milk you claimed to be bringing five hours ago? Still working on it? I found quite theatrical your slow creep toward the kitchen with a quick pirouette back toward

191

your bedroom once you thought you were out of my field of vision. Can you hear my slow clap? Because I'm not doing it.

Speaking of lies, statements such as "We're all out of water" make you seem silly. Out of water. Because we're being rationed all of a sudden. Did the marshmallow man fall into the ocean, contaminating it at the source, or did you just drink it all? I wish you could see my face right now.

Please let me know when I've come close to the maximum number of kisses I'm prequalified for. Frankly, the last four you gave me felt like charity. Who would have thought that it would take only a few short months after my birth for the passion to be gone. **Maybe no kiss is better than one given begrudgingly.** *The next time I cry out for repeated kisses, why not just shout "WAIT UNTIL MORNING, WENCH" from your bedroom. If I wake up the next day, you can give me one then.*

Regarding my napkin-sized blanket, I'll try to sleep without moving so that it doesn't fall off. Or maybe I'll buy growth hormones online so that my baby arms can adjust it without help. Even though I don't have a credit card and that's impossible, I'll figure out a way so you can sleep more peacefully.

If a sock comes off, I'll let my foot freeze and inevitably go dead. No need to put it back on correctly. Just shove it on sole side up and inside out.

I'll be so quiet at night that it'll be like you don't even have a kid. That's what you want, right?

I just have one more question: When I called for you specifically, did I stutter? Because I noticed that you sent Daddy in. Hmm, weird.

Anyway, I just want to let you know that I've put all that behind me and am willing to give you a fresh start. That's just the kind of person I am. A lover.

Lots of real actual love, HT

♦ ♦ ♦

Dear Honest Toddler,

My two-year-old has a fever and is refusing to let me take her temperature. What should I do?

—Worried Mother in Atlanta, Georgia

Dear Worried,

Toddlers sometimes have trouble giving, so if you want to take anything from your child, including a temperature, please submit a written request 48 hours in advance. The answer will probably be no.

Love, HT

14

Green Snot:
How to Treat Your Toddler's
Illnesses

Even the strongest toddler will eventually come into contact with a virus powerful enough to slow her down for a few days. I've heard that some parents actually enjoy the lethargic version of their under-the-weather child, but I'm going to reject this twisted rumor.

Medicine

The first thing you're going to be tempted to do when your angel's nose starts dripping highly viscous but edible liquid is to buy medicine. Medicine is a scam. It doesn't taste anything like the fruits pictured on the label and can burn holes in plastic. A class-action lawsuit by the children of the free world against the chefs behind these bitter recipes is in progress. Whether a medicine works or not is irrelevant when your child is unable and unwilling to ingest it. You may be asking yourself, "But why not? My child has licked more computer keyboards and DMV countertops than I can count.

Why won't he take this FDA-sanctioned poison?" You don't need to understand so much as you need to drop the idea entirely.

And while you're out in alleys, buying liquid drugs from shifty figures hiding in the shadows, ask yourself whether "Just say no" means anything to you. If you're buying homeopathic remedies, don't think you're any less guilty just because your dealer dresses like a yogi.

A spoonful of sugar does not help the medicine go down, but it is a most welcome substitute.

Popular Medicine Avoidance Methods

Toddlers will use many tactics to avoid swallowing pain:

- **Mouth Clamp:** self-explanatory. This shield cannot be pierced. Don't even think about holding your child's nose.
- **Sit-and-Spit:** This technique was made popular by an eighteen-month-old in Michigan and since then has spread like wildfire. It starts with faux compliance. When the parent figure lets down his guard, the child spits the medicine in their face or lets it drip out of her mouth. So funny.
- **Hawaiian Punch:** Only the boldest toddlers will attempt this masterful form of rebellion. As you bring the spoon, miniature cup, or plastic oral syringe toward your child's mouth, a chubby hand knocks not only the single dose of medicine but the entire bottle onto the floor. Problem solved.

Sneaky Medicine

It's wrong to hide medicine in your toddler's foods. Your child is not an elephant at the zoo. "Oh, I'm just sprinkling probiotics into this smoothie, my actions are harmless." No, they're not. Unless you're okay with your toddler sneaking mystery ingredients into your salads, please cease and desist.

Toddler-Approved Natural Medicine

If your toddler's health and emotional well-being are concerns of yours, look into natural medicine. Many of my friends play doctor, and we've developed holistic remedies to cure your child's ailments.

Runny Nose: Change into a long cotton shirt or dress that can double as a nose-wiping surface. This is far more convenient and environmentally friendly than Kleenex. Letting your child empty her head full of mucus on your person encourages family bonding and nasal healing.

Cough: Run a hot shower. Sit in the bathroom with your toddler, telling stories for several days. Bring a flashlight, snacks, and an iPad.

Irritability: Pick up your toddler and carry him around until you hear different.

Fatigue: See Irritability.

Most toddler ailments can be helped with attention, so just throw away your watch, phone, and keys and plan to be there as long as it takes. You'll be in a reclining position with your toddler until things look up. Put on some comfortable clothes and forget your agenda. If you start to get restless, remind yourself that love means sacrifice.

In conclusion, don't let your family doctor trick you into buying medicine. He or she is just trying to please the advertisers and earn a commission. Love, caring, and unlimited juice are what your toddler needs when she's feeling under the weather. The good news is that only one out of three of those costs money.

Homework: Taking care of a toddler is easy when you follow your heart and the directions provided in this chapter. The next time you run into your child's pediatrician, keep walking and pretend you don't recognize him.

• ◆ •

The Womb: A Review

I spent almost a year in this establishment and, for the most part, give it two fully formed thumbs up. The food, while not Zagat-rated, was wonderful all the same. Don't expect a fixed menu: soft serve and chorizo one day, a strict regimen of antacids the next. A quick thanks to Placenta, my concierge, for handling all of the dining arrangements. It's nice to know someone with connections. The accommodations are cozy but sparsely decorated; they really embraced a minimalist approach.

My only complaint was about the guests in the next room . . . an emotionally unstable woman whose constant chewing was almost impossible to tune out, and her manservant. Fortunately, my entire stay was comped.

The pool was enormous. All encompassing. I never left it.

I would visit this place again but I'd bring a towel as none were provided.

Check-out was a mess.

HT

• ◆ •

Dear Honest Toddler,

I've always wanted to know . . . what does a contraction feel like from the inside?

—Inquisitive in Massachusetts

Dear Inquisitive,

Contractions feel like increasingly urgent hugs from a damp person who may or may not be angry with you.

Warmly, HT

15

The Long Hello:
Birth

Back labor, Pitocin—yeah, yeah, we all know that birth was a difficult couple of minutes for you, but have you considered how the longest swim of his life has impacted your toddler? Perhaps your child's loud response or acting out is due to residual issues surrounding the labor experience.

Placenta

"What is a placenta?" you may be asking yourself. A placenta is a support person placed within the womb to keep your toddler comfortable in utero. A placenta's role is very complex. Its duties include concierge services, GPS, and catering. First and foremost, a placenta is a best friend. While other organs are typically stand-offish, a placenta is welcoming by nature and truly hospitable.

To understand the deep relationship your toddler had with his placenta, consider that the two of them spent almost a year as roommates in very tight quarters. You know, there isn't a lot to do in the womb. It's no Six Flags Magic Mountain. There's no lending library or Build-A-Bear. Placenta was your toddler's first and only source of love/entertainment. Respect that.

The next time your toddler cries out in the middle of the night, maybe it isn't just "nothing." Maybe your child misses her placenta.

Labor

The reason so many toddlers detest putting on tight sweaters, or shirts in general, is because of labor. Plunging one's large head through a hole that doesn't seem equipped to handle its diameter is all too reminiscent of the final moments in the birth canal. It was more than a bit smothering and uncomfortable. You've never been through it, so you can't quite understand.

No toddler knows beforehand that labor is going to happen. In my case, placenta tried to warn me, but I thought it was just being paranoid. Then one day . . . one day, the contractions started. Imagine the walls of your home, the inside of a waterbed, suddenly constricting around you, slowly at first, then with increasing frequency and strength. An abode that was once cozy is now downright stifling. A one-bedroom transforms into a studio apartment with a bed that pulls out of the wall. It's surreal.

Now add to that the sounds of muffled commotion from the outside. Your host's sweet, soothing voice is no longer singing to you; no, it's saying some crazy stuff. Swears. Screams. She is literally threatening the life and well-being of all people within earshot. As in real bodily harm. She's being specific, too. Rated-R-HBO-specific. This is Mother? It sounds like she's fighting the battle of her life. It's Armageddon out there, and you don't know whether to swim against the stream or go with it.

All at once the squeezing walls aren't just putting pressure on your small, naked body from the sides; they're pushing you down and out. It's time to leave, and you haven't even filled out a change-of-address form. You have no idea where you're going or who will meet you on the other side. Have you ever flown into a city without establishing a ride home from the airport? No. It would be unsettling. So is a one-way labor descent. As you get closer to the tunnel's end, you hear the voices getting louder. "PUSH!" You don't know whether they're talking to you or if your name is "Push"; it's all very confusing. Finally, at the end, you slip out into an ice-cold world of cotton blends and artificial lighting.

It's nice that people seem happy to see you. But the people. Jeez. Looking rough doesn't begin to describe the situation. Placenta is gone. The womb is gone. Yes, the food gets interesting, but the transition from inside to outside is a difficult one, and many toddlers still struggle to acclimate. If you suspect that your toddler is having a hard time assimilating, refer to the list below.

Signs That Your Toddler May Not Be Over the Birth Experience
1. **Trying to crawl back into your womb.** This is a fairly obvious indicator. He may understand that the tunnel is one-way, but that won't stop the determined child from trying to go against traffic when life gets overwhelming.
2. **Calling out for placenta in his sleep.** It may help to buy a placenta-shaped throw pillow.
3. **Building a blanket fort, filling it with water, and intentionally collapsing it around her.** Womb re-creation is normal.

In time, your toddler will come to accept his current lifestyle. Be patient and perhaps purchase a bed that resembles a uterus. Just an idea.

Adoption

"I didn't give birth to my toddler, he's adopted, does that mean that he won't resent me for his ejection from the womb?" Being born of the heart does not mean your toddler will shower you with gratitude, if that's what you're thinking. Please don't hold your breath waiting for some kind of thank-you card or Hallmark keepsake. You're a parent just like any other, and you won't get special treatment.

But you've made a wise choice. Every toddler deserves a forever family. Don't feel intimidated by parents who have known their toddlers from conception, because just look at the job they're doing. I mean really look at it. All you need to do to be a successful parent is follow your instincts. The very first time your instincts lie to you and say anything about leafy greens, abandon that particular frequency in your head.

You're a mom or dad now and the temptation to do things like link behavior and dessert is going to feel overwhelming at times. Philosophy calls this "evil." Resist it and try not to do Internet research. Quality time with your toddler is of pinnacle importance during the initial bonding period. Invest in some blankets for cuddling. Fill your home with balloons. You should already have crunchy snacks. Subscribe to a chocolate milk delivery service in your area.

During times like this, an adequate support system is vital so get a hammock for you and your small child to relax in after a long day at the park that you visit every day.

Toddlers just need to able to trust that you'll be there for them. Most mathematicians agree that "being there" means creating no more than a three inch distance. Grab a ruler if you're unsure.

General FAQ from Adoptive Parents

My toddler doesn't look like me, and people keep making a big deal. What should I do?

Answer: Lots of toddlers don't look like their parents; we consider these the lucky ones. Who wants to resemble the Time-Out Squad, anyway? I find both my parents beautiful in their special ways but am thrilled to have my own face.

Do I tell my toddler that she is adopted?

Answer: If you want to, you can. The one thing all toddlers want is to know that the people who mean the most to them will always be there, supporting and loving them. Once you assure them of Grandma and Grandpa's affection, they'll be fine.

Should I change my toddler's name?

Answer: I suggest letting your toddler choose his own name. Given the option, I would go by Dangerous Red. Just Danger, for short. Copyright pending, so don't use this.

Dear Honest Toddler,

On our last plane trip, my toddler told TSA that I had a gun. I did not. We were unable to board the plane and I was subjected to an invasive full-body search. How do I prevent something like this from happening again?

—Scared in Wichita, Kansas

Dear Scared,

LOL

Love, HT

16

Good Times:

Vacationing with Your Toddler

Did someone tell you that vacations are supposed to be relaxing? That's hilarious. Vacations are a chance for you to parent outside your comfort zone. If you can care for a toddler in a new place and without supplies from home, you're a true pro. See a vacation as a challenge, not as a gift to yourself, and you'll notice a dramatic improvement in your attitude and overall experience.

Packing

There's no such thing as minimalism when it comes to packing for a trip with small children. Whether you're going for two nights or fifteen, the basic rule of thumb is to bring everything. Diaper bag? No. Empty your toddler's drawers and closets into garbage bags. Not the kind intended for kitchen trash cans, buy the ones that landscapers use for leaves. Put all the toys into boxes and mail them ahead for your convenience. Before you leave, do a walk-through of your home. If you recognize anything, take it with you.

Transportation

The second step of any vacation is figuring out how you're going to transport your toddler and her personal belongings. Car? Plane? Boat? Large bird?

Airplanes

If your budget is limitless, I suggest going by air and flying first-class. It costs only ten dimes more than coach and features larger seats for your toddler to not sit in. There's nothing rich people love more than sitting in the first six rows of an aircraft with your baby-pie. Free in-flight entertainment! It has been well documented that strangers like observing children because of their innocence and general amazing qualities. If your child has a loud response on the plane, people will gather around and help comfort your toddler by making it rain Hershey's Kisses.

Something about being so high up in the air brings out people's generosity of spirit. You may want to walk your toddler down the plane's aisles and do a little trick-or-treating. It doesn't have to be Halloween; people will be excited to give your toddler whatever they have: gold coins, valuable stamps, TUMS tablets, anything. On planes, toddlers are like celebrities. Not the hated kind, whom people love to see failing in life; the beloved kind, like Richard Gere or Meryl Streep. Don't be surprised if someone asks for an autograph.

Bathrooms are present on all airplanes, but don't plan on using them. They're large enough for only one person to stand up in. If you have to change your toddler's diaper and you've taken my advice about flying first-class, you're in luck. Seats in this section have enough legroom for you to change the diaper on the floor. Use a barf bag to dispose of the soiled diaper. Your flight attendant will be happy to throw it out the plane's window and into the ozone layer.

Snacks

You can't count on airplanes to carry suitable food for your child. I've conducted my own research and found that most brands of crackers can survive high altitudes, but airlines are too belligerent to keep them stocked. I contacted American Airlines to get more information. Read the full transcript of the interview below:

> *Honest Toddler:* A square meal doesn't have to consist of the four food groups. It can also literally be a square. Crackers, for instance.
> *American Airlines:* Who is this?
> *Honest Toddler:* I'd like the name of the chef who created your beef-and-mushroom dish. It tastes like colic.
> *American Airlines:* We can't give out the names of our employees.
> *Honest Toddler:* Who told you that people like baked chips? They smell like foreclosure. Get regular ones.
> *American Airlines:* I'm going to have to let you go now.
> *Honest Toddler:* Have you considered distributing Ziploc bags of cereal upon boarding?

Due to a poor connection, the line went dead.

I have personally flown twice. The last time I screamed something along the lines of "We're all going to die," so I may or may not be one of the youngest people on the No-Fly List. It's temporary: When I turn sixteen, my case will be reviewed.

Happy flying!

Hotels

Have you ever fantasized about living in a one-room house with your family? Everyone sleeping, bathing, and eating in under five hundred square feet? So cozy together? This is hotel life. Every hotel room comes with a television, a remote control, a bathroom, a rug for free play, soap, lotion, several mirrors, a pad of paper, and at least one bed. Parents, if there is only one bed and you call the front desk for a Pack 'n Play, I hope you plan to sleep in it, because your toddler won't.

Hotel sleep is like home sleep but less. Forget everything you know about bedtime, because in hotels, kids don't fall asleep; they pass out around midnight and wake up at five A.M. You'll love living in a hotel. It's like being in an old-style log cabin with none of the beauty.

Winter Vacations

Snow is real and exists in many parts of the world. Take your toddler to see some snow, but know that you won't be hitting the slopes unless you have cloning technology. Even then, your toddler will want both of you. Most of the time in your winter wonderland will be spent helping your toddler in and out of snow pants, jackets, gloves, boots, hat, and scarf. Forget about the scarf.

If your toddler waits until she's fully dressed to notify you about a poo-poo, please do not make a big deal. One thing you should know about snow is that it's unnaturally cold. Your child will also eat it by the handful. Leave it alone.

Trips to the Beach

Beach vacations are the best. Water. Sun. Sand. Crying. You'll be thinking about this getaway for a long time. Prepare yourself for a day of fun-fun-fun by packing the following items.

1. Five-family multi-room tent or car-sized umbrella. Protect yourself from the beautiful, evil sun. Give it a chance, and it will end you.
2. Sunscreen. This is just for show. The sun is not afraid of yogurt. If you're self-conscious about the opinions of strangers, keep a bottle on hand to flash around.

3. Hundreds of sand toys.
4. Snacks for eight days.
5. Enough water and juice to fill a whale four times.

You may be curious about beach etiquette. The good news is, there is none. Don't interrupt your child's play for bathroom breaks. Peeing in the water is one of the privileges of time in nature. Poo can be buried in the sand with no consequences. Don't let anyone see you.

Everybody loves sand. And sand loves everybody. That's why it follows you home like a cute puppy. Long after your beach vacation is over, you'll find grains of sand in your food, private parts, and hair. Smile a little bit. They're like tiny memories.

Camping

Toddlers don't need help getting in touch with their inner animal, but camping allows them to express it freely. My spirit animal is a raccoon because of its destructiveness and our shared love of trash.

Camping is a lot like homelessness but intentional. Sleeping outside with only a zipper between you and the world might seem crazy, but don't worry—you won't sleep. It's difficult to get comfortable when the ground is your mattress, so your toddler will need to sleep on top of your body. You're like an air mattress, only instead of air, bones and blood.

There are no stoves in nature, so thankfully, there will be no cooking except of marshmallows. See it as a break from making your child's life more difficult than it needs to be. S'mores are fortified with many vitamins and minerals, so don't worry your big head about it. You'll have a great time.

- -
Homework: Vacations are the perfect time to bond and weep as a family. Take lots of photos, because you'll probably do it only once.
- -

Dear Daddy,

Before you go into your bedroom looking for your cell phone, I just want to let you know that I love you very much. I also want to remind you that I am a small child who is still learning about life and limits. You could say that I don't know my own strength.

Random question: Did you opt in on that mobile-phone insurance?

We are best friends, yes? Sometimes best friends make mistakes. I want you to learn a new word before you walk out of this room. The word is "forgiveness." People who forgive don't run around telling Grandma or Santa everything that happens in our home. They also don't hold grudges or withhold desserts.

I heard a phrase recently that resonated with me: "You can't take it with you." You literally can't take your cell phone with you anymore. Not unless you have a Ziploc bag for all of the pieces.

Love you, HT

17

Parents and Their Dangerous Vices: Learning Self-Control

Exhibit A: Parent's Night Out

Do you remember your life before children? Probably not. Your mind has blocked those memories because they are too painful. Here's a refresher.

You woke up around ten A.M. and completely missed dawn because there was no small child in the house. With no one to put a time limit on your shower, you stayed under the water for forty-five minutes and ruined the environment. Congrats! Now Mother Nature can't stand you. Your skin is dry and requires lotion. You have a full bottle because nobody has played with it.

Abundance leads to greed, and you become money-hungry. Fast-forward one year, and you're living a life of excess, throwing away your paychecks on designer clothes and sushi.

Having kids saved your life. It makes sense that you should sacrifice it for them. That's called "giving back." While some parents know that caring for children is a 24/7 job with no breaks, some adults—bad seeds—have created organized-crime units intended to lure otherwise adoring caregivers away from their posts. They distribute flyers with "Mom's Night Off" or "Daddy's Day Out" in bold Helvetica font. Don't fall for it.

What Is a Parent's Night Out?

A parent's night out is essentially a short-term abandonment that will not go unnoticed by your toddler. Take a parent's night out if you're willing to throw away all of the emotional investments you've made in your parent/child relationship. There is no guarantee that your toddler will be there when you decide to come back home, so think about that before you make your decision.

Those outings begin long before the adult leaves the house. The adrenaline rush that comes with foreknowledge of the crime to be committed will give you a dangerous natural high for days before the actual event. Symptoms include whistling and laughing too long. On the day of your scheduled negligence, you will overcompensate for your toddler's inevitable heartbreak with quality time. This is like opening an account in a bank to make up for planning to rob it later the same day. Ridiculous.

"But I'm not leaving until after my toddler is asleep!" So? You think that makes it right? Your toddler's needs don't end just because the moon is out. Not only are drinks of water, blanket help, and possible pajama changes almost certain, your toddler's ability to sleep depends on knowing you are always just a shrill yell away.

You really wouldn't like parent's-night-out events, anyway. Groups of delinquent parents usually just go for night walks and discuss homeowners' insurance. It sounds a lot more exciting than it is. Snacks are provided, but they're usually just chopped parsley.

The first parent's night out was in 1974, and the families involved are still suffering the aftereffects. The adult children are scared of the dark, and they all breathe through their mouths.

If someone you know asks you to attend a parent's night out, there are many ways to say no.

Turning Down a Parent's-Night-Out Invitation

Invitation: Hey! Would you like to join me in putting my toddler and family second?
Response: No, but have fun trying to rebuild the bridge of trust and connectivity that you have trampled upon, come morrow.

Invitation: A few friends and I know nothing about love. Care to join us next Thursday evening?
Response: No, thanks, I believe the children are our future. Teach them well and let them lead the way.

Invitation: I'm not sure our toddlers will have enough to talk about in therapy twenty years from now. Care to enrich their sessions this Friday night?
Response: Sounds tempting, but every night is family night in my humble abode.

Resisting the pressures of today's society isn't easy, but if you do resist, you'll be rewarded by your toddler. Not in thanks or words of kindness but via a general acknowledgment of your presence.

Tip: Avoiding making friends in the first place is one of the easiest ways to reduce parent's-night-out temptations.

A Stern Word About Babysitters

Ah, so you still need to have a night out or attend an important "work" meeting, and have decided to leave your toddler with a virtual stranger. You put an ad on Craigslist and picked the first person to apply without conducting a background check or even a simple interview. When your toddler reacts with fear at the prospect of being left with someone she has never seen in her life, you chalk it up to normal jitters. F.

I find it amazing that parents won't leave their cars unlocked in an underground garage but will hire babysitters. Are a few tons of steel more important than the twenty-five pounds of joy in your life? When you hire a sitter, you take a risk. Common sense should tell you that no one in her right mind would volunteer to spend time with your toddler. I mean, come on. Does this person like watching *Finding Nemo* on a loop that much? I don't think so. What is this person's motive? I'll tell you right now: FRIENDSHIP.

Babysitters are incredibly lonely people, but it is not your toddler's responsibility to pity a person nine times his age. It's embarrassing, really. When adults find themselves without a wolf pack, they often use babysitting as an emotional crutch. Toddlers are very busy people. The thought of playing therapist to someone who, more than anything, needs to read a Dr. Phil book is exhausting.

Babysitters, pull yourselves together. Most toddlers are nice enough, but we don't want to be best friends with someone who has credit-card debt. You understand. Have you tried line dancing? Some cardio with other adults might pick up your spirits and help you meet people. Toddlers aren't ready for this type of relationship. It's not us, it's you. It's definitely you. I'm sorry.

- -

Homework: Fire your toddler's babysitter. In lieu of a final paycheck, give her a piece of paper that says, "You are someone special."

- -

Exhibit B: Television

It's important to recognize how your pop-culture addictions impact your parenting abilities. We'll start with television. It's well known in the toddler community that when bedtime book pages are skimmed and the evening bath is overlooked, it's due to the TV. Curious how your favorite series has altered your parent/child relationship? Let's do the science.

The Office

I haven't seen much of this show, but what I did view was disturbing. The fact that adults spend all day at work only to come home and get excited about observing televised people in another office says a lot. The bulk of the program consists of monologues directed at the camera. I don't doubt that there are subliminal messages. No children are in *The Office*, and the lack of toddler representation speaks volumes. Do you watch *The Office*? There's a huge chance that you're a workaholic trying to get a fix. Tell me, what's so bad about being at home? If you find yourself drawn to this show, you need to quit your job. You're addicted.

Breaking Bad

Everything adults do comes down to money, and this show is no different. Basically, it's about one man's quest to pay his student loans. One of the main reasons I'm against daycare is that it leads to higher education. Two out of two humans have college debt, and many of them will end up on the wrong side of the law because of it. This show is meant to warn you away from the preschool system. If you're watching *Breaking Bad,* deep down, you agree.

Homeland

"Let's meet up soon!" "I've been meaning to call!" "I'm only going to eat one!" Everyone knows adults love to lie. Have you ever wondered how you got so good at it? Role models. *Homeland* is all about deception. Hundreds of people watch this show every week to learn lying skills, such as not blinking, keeping a steady tone, and insisting. If you watch this program but punish your toddler for the occasional harmless fib, your parenting style can be found under the category of "hypocrite." Admit it: You like lies. Bond with your toddler over this mutual interest rather than try to be someone you're not.

Game of Thrones

Being number one is everything, and *Game of Thrones* is all about this truth. In the show, people fight to hold on to their rightful status. Having multiple friends with Infant Sibling Disease, I am all too familiar with the battle. It's sad to see a friend go from the top of his game to being called the name of his brother or sister because the parents can't keep their kids straight. If you're an adult who loves *Game of Thrones*, your subconscious is trying to communicate with you. It's saying, "Don't have any more kids. One is enough."

Survivor

Being left to your own devices with a group of strangers who wouldn't hesitate to steal your last bread crust: Yep, sounds like a playdate to me. *Survivor* is about using your wits and strength to make it through an impossible unsupervised situation while your mother or father makes small talk with friends. Multiple challenges test the resolve of toddlers when they're on a forced-play excursion. Whether it's dealing with a hugger or a host who has only organic rice milk to drink, every young child knows what it's like to be in the battle of a lifetime. Don't just watch *Survivor*; learn from it and stop inviting people over.

Grey's Anatomy

Providing medical care is one of life's greatest callings. Watching doctors and nurses save lives is amazing. It's inspiring, really. Question: Do any of the medical professionals on *Grey's* ever question a patient's need for a Band-Aid? Do they ever say things like "Walk it off" or "You're okay, stop crying"? No. Real doctors know that some boo-boos are of an invisible, emotional nature. *Grey's Anatomy* exists to help insensitive parents learn how to be better first responders when a toddler needs immediate medical attention. You like it because you know you need help in that area.

Dancing with the Stars

I love the concept of *Dancing with the Stars*. Many parents miss getting dressed up and going out on the town. Once you have a toddler, those days are over. No, seriously, they're done. "I can just get a babysitter," and I can just get adopted out. Stop trying to outsource your duties and be present in your new life. In *Dancing with the Stars,* adults show the world that you can wear fancy clothes and dance all you want without leaving an enclosed familiar area. On the show, they're dancing in a studio, but the message is that you can do the same thing at home. There's no fun to be had out in the world that can't be had in your living room while your toddler watches closely. Even more good news: Toddlers love to dance!

The Walking Dead

On this show, you'll see a lot of poorly groomed creatures dragging their feet and mumbling incoherently. If you recognize one of these people as you at five in the morning, you have the insight of a wizard. *The Walking Dead* is about parents who, instead of going to sleep when their toddler does, stay up eating Cool Ranch Doritos until the wee hours of the morning. When they wake up with the sun to make their tyke's breakfast, they blame parenthood rather than poor choices for their terrible state of being. Having to live with a parent in this state of half-consciousness is disturbing. Imagine trying to enjoy a leisurely breakfast while an underworld-esque beast wearing pajama pants and a stained robe lumbers about, angrily spitting incoherent curses at the Tassimo. *The Walking Dead* has a simple message for you: You're scaring the children.

Mad Men

I haven't had a chance to see this show, but the title says everything I need to know. Angry fathers are an epidemic these days. You give one cell phone a little bath, and it's as if the world is coming to an end. Daddies, you need to learn to be more flexible. If someone draws back the shower curtain (who said you could shower alone, anyway?) to regard your full body-hair carpet, this isn't a reason to scream. Falling to the tub floor and pulling the curtain down with you is also quite melodramatic. Fathers without enough patience for normal toddler behavior, like DVD snapping, need to reevaluate what truly matters in life. Hint: It's not your iPad having an uncracked screen, it's kids. Kids matter. It may help if you change the personal pronouns you attach to these trinkets. More "ours," less "mine."

Parks and Recreation

This is another show I haven't caught, but I feel qualified to make an assessment. Ask me how many days it's been since I've been on a slide or felt the wind blow through my hair on the swings. Too many to count. Parents, the park is free. There are several in every city. Why is it so hard to make visits a twice- or thrice-daily practice? As part of my work in politics, I'm constantly lobbying for a minimum requirement of forty hours of jungle-gym time per week for every toddler. I know there's no Wi-Fi at most parks, and you hate half the parents there, but make this regular sacrifice for your child, and I promise it will pay off tenfold. If you enjoy *Parks and Recreation,* it's because you feel guilty. Make a change.

Exhibit C: Bad Food

People often knock toddlers for their food habits, but when you consider what parents eat on a regular basis, young children don't seem so crazy. What the foodie culture deems cool affects what ends up on toddlers' plates, so analyzing trends is a must if we're going to be proactive about meltdown prevention. Dinnertime is painful enough without the constant tide of bizarre fads.

As I become acquainted with the culinary world of adults, I find myself crying more and more. These aren't tears of sadness but of disappointment and anger. In this world, it seems less important that a dish retain simple deliciousness and more important that it is impressive, expensive, complicated, or rare. The following dishes are not fit for toddler consumption. Please show some respect and break the addiction.

Bruschetta

Bruschetta looks like someone tried to get a pizza recipe over the phone but only heard every fifth word. A mini-toast coaster topped with a tomato salad. What is this? The original recipe for toast is flawless. There are very few condiments that go well with bread. See below.

- Butter
- Occasional jam
- Cream cheese when requested
- Generous Nutella

None of these is interchangeable with chopped vegetables. Admit that you make bruschetta only when you are trying to impress people you fear and hate.

Coleslaw

Once upon a time, a bold fool said to himself, "Salad isn't terrible enough; let's increase its surface area tenfold." If someone you love has ever used an *ice-cream scoop* to plop a dripping pile of this stringy mess on your plate next to a hot dog, you've been through too much. Before coleslaw was invented, picnics were happy, carefree events for toddlers. It was a time when we could run through the sprinklers in our swimsuits without fear of side dishes.

Vegetables have never saved anyone's life, yet grown-ups stand convinced of their healing powers. My question to you is this: If vegetables help us grow strong, why are they themselves so weak? It's okay to challenge what you've been told all your life.

Caramelized Onions

I'd like to meet the person who named this dish. Having had caramel on multiple occasions, I find it interesting that we'd name burned, soggy onion slices after it. While adults get very giddy over the prospect of having eight or ten of these on top of whatever they're eating, your toddler would rather watch Rick Steves wander through Europe.

Extended Cooking

Slow-roasted. Aged. Braised. Did you just pee in your pants from excitement? Nothing gets an adult's heart beating quickly like knowing food has been cooking for months. I believe this is an ego trip: "My food has been preparing itself for me since the beginning of time. I must have royal blood." Relax, you're a rat-faced commoner like the rest of us. There is absolutely nothing special about meat that has been hanging in a closet or rotating on a spit for six years. Evidence? Hot dogs take under a minute to prepare and are one of the most coveted foods on the planet.

The older a cheese is, the more willing a grown-up is to take out a microloan to pay for it. Adults run each other over, looking for the most rotten triangle. That doesn't make any sense, especially considering the faces made by so many mothers and fathers when they find partially consumed meals aging around the house. Oh, that yogurt behind the couch was just fermenting into goodness! See how crazy it sounds?

No toddler no cry . . . unless you own a slow cooker. These devices have boomed in popularity, and hundreds of websites have created "recipes the whole family will love." Do families include toddlers? Slow cookers promise you a delicious meal that you can start in the morning and slop over some rice come dinnertime. There is nothing appealing about the gradual breakdown of individual ingredients over an eight-hour time period. If you have a slow cooker, please convert it to scrap metal or designate it for chocolate-melting purposes only.

It's my hope that with proper education, the extended-cooking trend will simmer itself into ash. Remember, your toddler is impressed not with the time that goes into a meal but with the Pop-Tart that comes out of it.

All-Natural Foods

Poop is natural, but would you eat it? (More than once?) We have to stop judging food by whether it is natural and start letting each food stand on its own merit. If you worry about chemicals in food, the great news is you don't have to anymore. I asked my resident scientist an important question a few days ago: What is a chemical? Her answer will shock you: "A chemical is a flavor enhancement from the earth."

The fear of artificial ingredients is due to a simple misunderstanding. When a food doesn't have flavors of its own, it has to borrow flavors from another food. Some people call this artificial; I call it giving back. If a food can't find a sponsor, sometimes a lab will make it a prosthetic free of charge. This charity should be not feared but admired.

Now that we have that squared away, let's move on to so-called artificial colors. Everybody loves red drinks, but parents, especially mothers, believe that red is a dangerous color. Whether it's red, blue, orange, purple, or yellow juice, parents need not worry, because all of these colors can be found in nature via a rainbow. Look in the sky after it rains, and you'll see various colors stacked in half-circles. These hues are made by Mother Earth herself. Red drink, therefore, is as good for your toddler as a bunch of grapes.

A toddler's spirits sink a little bit when she sees her parents reading food labels in the grocery store. One minute you think you're going to get those peanut-butter-cake-cereal balls, and the next minute the goodness is being placed back on the shelf. Parents, spend less time reading the words and numbers on the label, and take a few minutes to look at the picture on the front. You'll see that it tells a beautiful story. Let the cartoon images speak to your inner child. Now put the box in your cart, pay for it, and take it home. You've done great.

Chips have mothers clutching their pears in fear. If you think of chips as very small, intense pieces of toast, you'll find it easier to serve them to your toddler as an anytime food. The crunch can be intimidating, but if your young child can handle it, so can you. Another benefit of eating chips daily is that they polish your toddler's teeth with their rough edges, as well as building jaw strength. Whether they're in triangle or circle form, these foods are extremely healthy. The next time you see a chip, apologize for stereotyping.

Peeps! These Easter classics are an example of how the natural-foods craze is hurting everyone. Are Peeps a fruit? No, they're a tribute to an endangered species. Food isn't just about eating things that grow on trees; sometimes it's about remembrance. When was the last time you saw a pink rabbit? Exactly. They're almost gone. Eating Peeps in homage is how you can make a difference.

Blogs on the Internet will tell you all kinds of crazy things about what's natural and what's not. At the end of the day, none of these people know what they're talking about. Nobody checks ID before a person starts a website and begins sharing ideas about what foods are okay for kids. Oh, it's the FDA? Who cares. Three letters doesn't make you the king of nutrition. To know if something is natural or not, taste it. Your body is rigged to cooperate: If your tongue says yes, trust that the rest of the body will be on board.

Weird Bread

Normal bread is made of flour and water. Don't let the grocery-store clerks pressure you into trying anything exotic.

How to Tell If a Bread Is Normal

1. Uniformity of white color. Pick a slice from the middle. It should look like a cloud blessed by an archangel.
2. No spots, specks, bumps, or mysterious abnormalities. Rub your tongue over a piece of the bread. Hopefully, it feels like you're licking a down comforter. If you've never licked a comforter or any blanket, what have you been doing with your life? Go experience something.
3. Search the bread for bombs: nuts, raisins, and seeds. They're called bombs because if you accidentally eat one, you'll feel like your life is over.
4. Ask someone who works at the store if the bread has been featured on any food blogs lately. If it has, that's a big red flag. Pass.
5. Drop bread to the floor. You shouldn't hear anything as it touches down. If there's a loud thud or dent in the linoleum, chances are you've picked up something made with a trendy flour, like rice or oat.

Exhibit D: Lies

Parents will go on and on about the need to tell the truth, but a recent study just reported that 100 percent of them lie. They lie to their bosses, their friends, themselves, but worst of all, parents lie to their toddlers. You don't know how crazy and desperate you look when you spin a story about leprechauns telling you that cauliflower is delicious.

"Vegetables Will Make You Strong"

This lie is coming apart at the seams as we speak. It's ridiculous. When I see a pea lift anything over its head or an orange bell pepper break a cement block, I will believe that vegetables can impart strength. They're not even powerful enough to taste good. They have little to no influence in the snack world and are hated by their closest relatives (fruit). When someone can't get along with the people in his inner circle, that should give you pause.

I'm not a licensed doctor, but I have noticed that toddlers feel most powerful after eating doughnuts. Also, after some red drink, most toddlers can fly. I mean, they can't fly, but they can definitely glide. Maybe not glide, but for sure they can get some decent air when jumping down a flight of stairs. Vegetables are strong enough to make children cry, but no one should praise a bully. Bottom line, parents, if you want to be respected in your home, bury this lie along with all the veggies in your crisper. Deep.

"I'm Going Right to Sleep"

You know you've said it. Your punkin is having a hard time accepting that she needs to be in bed. "Why should I be going to sleep when the party's still bumping?" your toddler thinks. So you say it: "I'm going to sleep, too." Stop. Just stop. You don't think your toddler hears and smells popcorn popping from his bed? Is he supposed to believe that popcorn is for snack time tomorrow? And the sounds of Dove bars being unwrapped? Hmm? Television programs booming from the family room—laugh tracks, high-speed chases, GUNSHOTS—yes, we hear it all.

Toddlers know that the moment their heads hit the pillow, you release balloons and unwrap a cake. We are perfectly aware that when we're trapped in our rooms, wearing the wrong pajamas, you are eating a second, more desirable dinner. Why else would you rush us off to sleep? So reluctant to read books, so often replacing bath time with a baby-wipe scrub-down. We're onto you. Parents, you look terribly exhausted every single morning, and it's because you stay up until two A.M., looking at wavy hair on Pinterest and eating Almond Joys. "I'm going right to bed." Yeah, right.

"Soda Is Spicy"

Thanks to my now favorite uncle, I recently had the opportunity to sample orange Crush. I don't know what kind of oranges this miracle beverage comes from—mandarin in heavy syrup, I imagine—but it was like riding a carbonated high-fructose wave with dolphins all around, and I loved every second of it. After my mind stopped screaming and my eyesight returned to normal, my exhilaration turned to anger as I realized how many sips of soda I've backed down from after being told, "Oh, no no, it's spicy." That's how you share, huh? I hope you feel awful.

"I'm Not Eating Anything"

Every single toddler on the planet knows what it's like to have a parent come around a corner with chocolate breath. When asked what they were eating, the parent simply says, "Nothing," and tries to change the subject. Substitute chocolate for Hot Pockets if you must; you are missing the point. You're hiding food and lying about it. It is in no way okay for you to have a secret stash of snacks. You add insult to injury when you consume goodies in your toddler's face and then concoct the shakiest cover-up of your life. It's obvious that there is something terribly wrong with you.

"There's Nothing on Top of the Fridge"

YEAH, RIGHT. Then how come every single time your toddler turns around unexpectedly, you're putting something up there? What is it? Bubbles? Gum? Today is the day when you put a ladder against the fridge and let your toddler see for herself. It must be done. End these lies, and for once show your toddler some basic respect.

"We'll See/Maybe Tomorrow"

The phrases "We'll see" and "Maybe tomorrow" mean "No" and "Never." Parents, I don't think the issue is that you're afraid to say what you mean; I think it's that you know you're wrong for saying it and want to avoid a legitimate confrontation. What is your toddler asking for? A diamond-encrusted watch, or to go out and buy some applesauce? I know driving to the store and spending $4.50

on a fruit-based snack is daunting, but perhaps instead of saying "Maybe tomorrow," you can take a very small step outside of your comfort zone and make your toddler's day. I just . . . I just can't.

"I'm Going to Give You One More Chance"

This is one of my personal favorites. Imagine me sitting barefoot in the front entry, with my dad trying his darnedest to get us out the door. I've been asked to put on my shoes. "I'm going to give you one more chance." Are you sure? Just one more? Or maybe two? Or maybe ten, until you come over and put my shoes on for me. HAHAHAHA! You guys are so funny when you want to be.

"I'm Going to Pull This Car Over"

Backseat mayhem. Toddlers are known for getting crazy in moving vehicles. Taking off shoes, socks, and (somehow) shirts, throwing food, thrashing about—it's all part of the lifestyle. Don't take it personally, even though sometimes you should. When you make it about you, it's easy to get overwhelmed and start saying things you don't mean, like "I'm going to pull the car over." We all know you're not going to exit the freeway and stop the car in some warehouse district. Even if you did, what then? Would you give your toddler a stern talking-to? Chances are, she can't hear you over her inner tornado. Just keep driving. Pass back some fruit snacks if you have them, but keep driving.

"Santa Can See You"

This one is pretty tricky. Most toddlers have a very delicate relationship with Father Christmas and are aware of his surveillance techniques. What parents are unaware of is that the North Pole and the Toddler Council of Everlasting Gloriousness signed a treaty in 1983, allowing for a daily "no watch" period between three P.M. and seven P.M. local time, with summers off. Santa's approval rating in the early eighties had reached an all-time low due to discouraged toddlers, and this agreement was instrumental in restoring holiday cheer and incentivizing good behavior by making the nice list more attainable. So the next time you tell your toddler "Santa can see you," take a look at the clock. Are you sure?

- -

Homework: Practice telling the truth. It might burn your mouth on the first few tries, but it will get easier with regular practice.

- -

Dear Honest Toddler,

Sometimes when I come back from the grocery store I can't open the door in time and have small accidents. Am I truly potty-trained? If not, can I really expect my toddler to be potty trained?

—Trying Not to Be a Hypocrite in Maryland

Dear Hypocrite,

No and no.

Love, HT

18

Potty Training Simplified/Eliminated

When you think about it, although I doubt you will, it is unfair to ask your child to change the lifestyle she has become accustomed to. Your son is but a boy, your daughter just a girl. I'm going to cut to the chase: Learning to use the toilet is too hard for your child. Forget everything you think you know about the practice and absorb the wisdom below.

Common Potty-Training Beliefs CHALLENGED

1. If you throw toddlers in big-kid underwear, they'll eventually get so tired of making messes that they'll train themselves. **False:** Toddlers are more disgusted by baby arugula than by their own solid waste.
2. Every president of the United States was potty-trained. **False:** Grover Cleveland and Abraham Lincoln were both respected U.S. presidents and NOT potty-trained.
3. Without potty training, your toddler will never get full-time work. **False:** Changing tables can be found in 90 percent of office bathrooms, and most have a weight capacity of two hundred pounds.
4. Potty training is difficult and can traumatize an entire family. **True.**
5. Potty-training accidents are easy to clean out of pint-sized

underwear. **False:** You can wash out poo, but you can't wash out hopelessness. Guess which one has a longer-lasting scent.

There comes a time in all parents' lives when they think it's okay to start potty-training their toddler. What's so funny is that it's impossible. Pee-pee is like eyesight; you can't control how or when it comes out of you. Adults get good at predicting number ones and twos, but nobody is "potty-trained," so to speak. It's an urban myth that children possess the capability for the complex math required to foretell their emissions. The gift of prophecy is rare. Do not make your toddler feel bad for not being blessed with it.

> *"But I know kids who are potty-trained."* No, you don't. Either you were lied to, or you heard what you wanted to hear. It's not unusual for toddlers in some communities to fake being potty-trained for M&M's. These children end up with Pavlov syndrome and, in the future, would probably rob a bank if someone promised them gummy bears. Sad.

> *"I was potty-trained as a toddler."* Also untrue. Do you remember being potty-trained? What shirt were you wearing at the time? That's what I thought. Find the person/people who lied to you, and ask why.

> *"I read a book that told me toddlers can be potty-trained. There's one that says kids can be potty-trained in three days."* Three days. You can't even make cheese in three days. Potty-training books are extremely useful: makeshift gum, doorstops. The possibilities are endless!

Potty-Training Charts

Data doesn't mean much to toddlers, and most don't know what a bar graph is. If you've purchased poster board and are trying to motivate your child with stickers or check marks, you've already lost. Toddlers will accept handouts without a doubt, and may play your game if it'll earn applause, but don't expect a long-term commitment.

I urge you not to get excited when your toddler follows your poop-and-pee schedule for a few days. Keep those diapers nearby, because she's just having fun with your heart. Unless you're currently a toddler, you'll find it hard to comprehend how totally adorable it is to see a parent enter into a fit of glee over an ideally placed piece of excrement or puddle of yellow. Don't hate the player, hate the game.

Stickers

It is unfair to use stickers in your potty manipulations, because young children cannot resist them. Toddlers feel for stickers what some adults feel for McRibs: They're elusive, rare, and magical. You know from your baby's love of Band-Aids that adhesives have a special place in the hearts of the under-three. Tampering with this vice is dangerous and can backfire, resulting in extended behavioral regressions. The space between a toddler and her stickers is a dangerous place to plant oneself. You have been warned.

Big-Kid Undies

First of all, LOL. Second . . . why? What is the appeal in making the switch from super-comfortable diapers to "big-kid underwear"? The whole concept of cotton single-ply coverings is lost on children. You're telling me, given the choice, that adults wouldn't prefer a highly absorbent self-cleaning sheath over their danger zone? One that gets switched out several times a day for maximum comfort? If I understand correctly, cotton pantaloons are rotated once every twenty-four hours. They are then washed and dried, and the cycle begins all over again? Sounds lovely.

Diapers come in a variety of styles, and the designs can be quite eye-catching! Underwear is usually beige and retains stains for maximum shaming. Put your toddler in undies made of natural fibers if you're trying to make enemies out of strangers. In the event of a public accident, these "down there" handkerchiefs will flip out a mud nugget like a reluctant hammock. I sincerely hope you're not in a crowded restaurant when that golf ball falls out of your child's pants leg. If you let it, underwear will do you dirty over and over. Diapers cost next to nothing, are available in stores nationwide, protect your reputation, and know the meaning of loyalty. Make the right choice.

Plastic Sheets

The idea that a small child, still relatively new to earth, can control his intestines during the day is funny. The idea that he can control them at night while unconscious is insane. I suppose you also think toddlers can pick up a second language during REM sleep? Why not change the oil in your car, too? Just to be clear, you are raising a human child, not an otherworld magical goblin with supernatural powers. But if there's one thing parents are never short on, it's schemes.

Once upon a time, an impulsive adult had a thought: "I'd love to save ten cents a night on diapers." From this money-hungry seed came a product: plastic fitted sheets that can be used in lieu of disposable diapers. These saran wrap–style bed fittings prevent mattresses from being ruined and can be rinsed off with a hose in the front yard. Yes, your toddler will wake up in a cold three-inch-deep puddle of ammonia, but look at you saving $2.80 a month! WOW. What will you do with the cash influx? Buy some hot-dog buns? SAD.

If you believe that obedience of the people in your charge is worth their discomfort and bad living conditions, go make friends with some war criminals, because you have a ton in common.

Sleeping on a plastic mat feels a lot like sleeping on a plastic mat. I imagine prison inmates would be able to describe it better.

Training Pants

These posers think they can walk the fence when it comes to potty training, but at the end of the day, they're a gateway drug to underwear. Keep them away from your toddler unless you enjoy scraping dirt sewage out of cloth with your bare hands. That's what you'll have to do.

Dangerous Comparisons

The number one reason parents lose their minds over potty training is peer pressure. If I've said it once, I've said it a hundred times: Your friends are deadweight when it comes to raising a happy toddler. Who cares what they've strong-armed their children into doing? Sixty percent of what comes out of the mouths of your "friends" are lies; the other 40 percent is pure nonsense. Don't let people who probably secretly dislike you play a part in your parenting choices.

If your friends ask you about your toddler's potty-training status, feel free to use any of the answers below to either shut them up or put them in their place.

Frenemy: My six-month-old just started signing when she needs to pee. How is your Nora doing?
You: Your dumb baby sounds like a dummy.

Frenemy: I'm so proud of my eleven-month-old! She's not even one and is fully potty-trained. What about Hadley? I can give you some advice.
You: The only thing you need to give me is three feet of distance unless you love throat punches.

Frenemy: What do you think about the latest potty-training board book?

You: I don't think about it at all. It's called love. Try it sometime.

You're asking yourself: When is the right time to begin potty training, then? Never. You didn't have to teach your toddler how to walk. She just picked it up. Nobody taught him to steal. He learned on his own. If your toddler ever wants to start using a toilet, she'll start. I know I say this all the time, but it's none of your business.

- -

Homework: Distance yourself from people who make you feel self-conscious about your toddler's potty status. Stock up on diapers.

- -

Conclusion:

You've Come a Long Way

When you opened this book, you knew next to nothing about toddlers. By now, the only thing stopping you from being a wonderful parent, caregiver, grandparent, or friend to a small person is YOU. We don't ask for much. Just everything. Once you let go, life will reward you with more opportunities to let go of even more. It'll all be worth it when your toddler wraps her arms around your neck and tenderly whispers, "I had an accident."

I'm proud of you.

Note to Toddlers

Don't change a thing.

Afterword

It is with much hesitation that I now allow my mother to speak directly to parents. Many of her "ideas" have been attempts to stifle my voice, but she has promised me churros, so you know.

Dear Reader,

First, thank you for purchasing this book. You've brought me one step closer to my dream of hiring a full-time au pair. Just kidding. Not really.

Being a parent is incredible. My favorite parts, probably much like yours, are the thirty seconds during mealtimes when everyone is eating happily, morning snuggles, and nap time.

HT has always been a very sweet child, but the dawn of toddlerhood was a transformation that took me by surprise. While not my first child, HT was the first to empty a box of cereal into a toilet and unwrap a fifty-count box of tampons. I like to use the word "spirited."

Anyone who spends a significant amount of time with toddlers knows how they can transport you from heaven to hell and back again. Their faces are works of angelic beauty, and their antics drive many of us to start purchasing wine in cardboard containers for ease of storage. Every single day, I'm baffled by the stark contrast between a giggle that sounds like bejeweled sparkling droplets of liquid gold dancing on a lake, and a scream that would

*curdle the breast milk of nearby lactating women. I love my tod-
dler. Sometimes I look at that beautiful young face and ask, "From
whence did you come, evil spirit?" But the love is there.*

*I like to think of parenting a toddler as a journey into one's
psyche. It feels like a form of unethical therapy; it exposes your
weaknesses and shines light on your strengths but also leaves you
slightly crippled and unable to function properly. As a parent, you
pick up lots of coping mechanisms, like compulsive eating, hum-
ming to yourself, and nail-biting, just to make it through bedtime.*

*The wild thing is, I wouldn't change a thing (other than hiring
the au pair I talked about before). HT is crazy, but because I'm
now infected with the same strain of crazy, it's all good. If I'm not
mistaken, that's also how vaccines work.*

*I must go and find some churros now. I hope you have a smooth,
loud response–free day. Remember, they won't be toddlers forever.
And you'll miss it.*

—Bunmi Laditan

Acknowledgments

To my family, thank you for all the love, support, and seemingly endless supply of the Baby-Sitters Club books.

To my brilliant and ever patient agent, Rachel Sussman of Chalberg & Sussman, thank you for believing in me as a writer. You are the definition of compassionate professionalism.

To Kate Mills of Orion Books, your early enthusiasm for this book will never be forgotten. Thank you. Also, if the offer to be paid in jelly beans is still good, I might be interested.

To Kara Watson at Scribner, you are a tireless and dedicated wordsmith. Thank you for helping me stay true to my voice, and being flexible with the deadlines.

To Kate Cassaday of HarperCollins Canada, from our very first phone call, I knew I had to work with you. You just *got* it, even before I did.

Thank you.